6.50

PS #4 1-22-65

Essay Index

ADVENTURE OR EXPERIENCE

ADVENTURE OR EXPERIENCE

FOUR ESSAYS
ON CERTAIN WRITERS AND READERS
OF NOVELS

By

DOROTHY BREWSTER
AND
ANGUS BURRELL
Assistant Professors in Columbia University

Essay Index

BOOKS FOR LIBRARIES PRESS, INC.
FREEPORT, NEW YORK

First published 1930
Reprinted 1967

PRINTED IN THE UNITED STATES OF AMERICA

CONTENTS

INTRODUCTION

SEVERAL years ago the authors of the following essays published *Dead Reckonings in Fiction,* a volume of criticism concerned with modern fiction and the questions involved in its evaluation. They felt at that time uncertain about critical standards, distrusting the old and accepted formulas, and curious but unconvinced about new theories—rather at sea, in fact. Hence their choice of a nautical title: "dead reckoning" being a way of navigating without sights when the sky is overcast or the horizon blurred. The current disturbances (1930) have arisen out of little beyond the hysteria of amateur navigators who mistake their own tea-pot turmoil for an oceanic upheaval. The authors feel encouraged and confirmed in their dogmatic assertion of the tentativeness of all critical values. The essays on Gissing, on Virginia Woolf, and on several novels by Maugham, Bennett, and Mann are similar in point of view and method to those in *Dead Reckonings in Fiction.* The last chapter explores the reader's relation to novels with the aid of two or three hundred students who have reflected upon their own reading experience. These exercises

1

in introspection and retrospection are a challenge to the formulators of values. They suggest that the reading of fiction may be either an adventure or an experience; and that in both cases there are implications too generally disregarded by critics.

Adventures are happenings that come to us or that we go out and seek; things we do or have done to us. When we realize the significance of an adventure, it becomes an experience. And it need not be our own adventure. It is less important for writers to have adventure than to have a realization of what adventure means. Thackeray would have had neither time nor energy, what with all the other characters he was creating, to live even one-tenth of Becky Sharp's life. Yet Thackeray knew Becky. While he never could have paralleled her adventurous life, he could and did experience her. She was born, that is, out of Thackeray's large and reflective experience of life. Balzac spent three or four unadventurous years of his youth as a lawyer's clerk, as a publisher, as a student. Then he locked himself into his room and wrote, experiencing with intensity adventurous lives by the hundred. "His own experience consisted of a passionate participation in the pleasures of the characters he created. For he himself threw the ten louis d'or on to the gaming-table, he himself stood trembling as the roulette wheel turned, he himself it was who

2

with feverish fingers clutched the winnings; it was he himself who had a wonderful theatrical success, who stormed the heights with his brigade, who convulsed the stock market with his machinations.'' * When he had nothing but a loaf of bread in his garret for his dinner, he drew a circle in chalk on his table to represent a plate; within the circle he wrote the name of some delectable dish; and the bread became that dish, and he experienced exquisite delights of dining, where nine-tenths of the people able to buy such food would have had mere adventures in consumption. Of the adventures of Gissing's youth, one at least bore fruit in experience. To steal a petty sum and be found out and punished has happened to thousands of boys and has remained just an unlucky episode. To Gissing it was an experience, only torturingly half-realized, which opened up that realm of conflict and suffering to be found in his novels. He shrank from more adventures; for him one was more than enough. Jane Austen lived in a very quiet, restricted way. The fact that she was no adventurer was all to her advantage as a novelist. There was not much of the social activity that passed before her in her mother's drawing-room that she did not make her own through experience. She may have been protected from life—to paraphrase Mr. Chesterton—

* Stefan Zweig. *Three Masters: Balzac.*

but there was very little of life that was protected from Jane Austen.

Adventures of their own may swamp writers in blind feeling rather than emancipate them in insight. It is the part of reflection, of imagination, to supplement in idea, in fancy, what has lacked in deed. Our experience begins where the blindness of adventure leaves off. Doing and realization seem in their nature for the most part to be antithetical. Not always. One thinks of Conrad, who adventured for twenty years and realized the significance of his adventures for twenty more. But most would-be writers who feel it necessary to rush up and down across the face of the waters and the earth discover that their energy and talent have been completely spent in adventuring. And if a man has fulfilled himself in this way, what energy or instigation has he left for a rehearsal in words? But if a man has not fulfilled himself, he may be impelled to complete himself in creation. We cannot of course be certain just how fully the urge to creation grows out of denial and not out of fulfillment. Bunyan, denied the activities of the ordinary citizen, wrote *Pilgrim's Progress* in jail; and Dante was impelled to write a "comedy" only when his worldly career was a consummate failure. Where life is perfect fulfillment, where the adventure of life is complete, there are no novelists, no poets. Lacking the perfect fulfillment of Paradise and the blinding narcotic of adventure, mortal poets have made of their dreams an earthly paradise or an inferno. Out of adventure comes silence; of their experience was born their dream.*

What has been said of the writers has its application to the readers of fiction, to whom a novel may be adventure or experience. Light on the distinction will come from what the readers quoted in the last chapter tell of themselves. And in the telling they pose a problem for the critic; for the same novel may be only an adventure to one reader, and a profound experience to another. How can criticism assess the value of that novel? Is there any value independent of the reader's response? Or is the value somehow created out of the multitude of responses?

* Quoted in part from an article by Angus Burrell, published in *MS.*, August, 1930.

CHAPTER I
GEORGE GISSING:
RELEASE THROUGH FICTION?

I

GEORGE GISSING is now remembered chiefly for his gloomy realistic novel, *New Grub Street;* and for his famous long essay, *The Private Papers of Henry Ryecroft,* in which he wistfully contrasts the life he has lived with a life he wished he might have had, and generally unburdens his soul in reflections about his own unhappy temperament in conflict with a not too friendly age. A third book should be mentioned—*By the Ionian Sea,* an account of a visit to Southern Italy. If to these three books, we add two more—*Charles Dickens,* a critical appreciation, and *Veranilda,* an historical romance of the Roman-Gothic conflicts of the sixth century, we suggest at once the scope of Gissing's interests and achievements.

In this list we have mentioned only one novel, *New Grub Street.* But George Gissing spent most of his life writing novels, and, if we exclude *Veranilda,* all of them present recurring themes. Some of these recurrent patterns are: first, the vicissitudes of young men with good minds and no money, their resentful attitude towards society, their eventual compromise or failure; second, either an absurdly sentimental over-

evaluation of women, or the most vindictive and
unjust under-evaluation; third, heroes exhibiting
flights from sex adjustments (often very cleverly
rationalized) or flights into sex relationships that
are usually disastrous.

There is nothing very remarkable in the fact
that a novelist should deal with money—or the
lack of it—and with love. Most novelists do. But
in many novels the problems involved are accepted as being the problems wholly of the characters. Theodore Dreiser's heroes are often ob-
sessed with money and with sex, and we believe
that their problems are their own, not Theodore
Dreiser's. In George Gissing's world we feel
that the heroes are often merely the protago-
nists for Gissing's own problems. This is to say
that Gissing is a betrayingly autobiographical
novelist (which is generally conceded); and this
is only another way of saying that Gissing is an
imperfect novelist, in that he never quite suc-
ceeds in presenting his characters with the ob-
jectivity that makes the reader believe in these
people as living their own lives in their own
world—propelled by their own inner natures.
Virginia Woolf has quite justly said: "For
Gissing is one of those imperfect novelists
through whose books one sees the life of the
author faintly covered by the lives of fictitious
people. . . . With such writers we establish a
personal rather than an artistic relationship."

And it is this "personal" relationship that we are trying to make clear in this chapter. Moreover, Mr. A. C. Gissing, a son of the author, writes in the Preface to *Selections, Autobiographical and Imaginative*: "There is no writer of fiction, that I know of, whose works are fuller of autobiographical material than are those of my father, or whose characters throw more light upon various aspects of their author's mind."

In a sense it is true that all fiction is nourished upon the writer's own conflicts. But there are some novelists whose characters walk off on legs of their own and flourish with a life distinctly theirs. Such novelists get so completely outside their material as to throw their work off into a realm where it moves in an orbit of its own. Arnold Bennett does precisely this in his great novel, *The Old Wives' Tale*. With such a novel there is usually no desire on the reader's part to explore the possible relationship between the author and his characters. One feels that Constance and Sophia Baines are completely realized in their own world; that in a sense they have no concern whatever with Arnold Bennett and that, still in a sense, he has nothing further to do with them. This seems to be true even of such obviously autobiographical novels as *The Way of All Flesh* and *Mary Olivier*. But there are other novels that tease us constantly with hints of below-the-surface adhesions; that are not wholly free of their creators. If we could trace the relationship we should understand better both the man and his books. George Gissing and his novels belong particularly in this latter category.

It is almost impossible to think of Gissing's work without reflecting about the man himself; and of this is generated a drama beyond the events of the stories. In Conrad, the part played by sea and ships; the lawyers and the inns-of-court in Galsworthy; patients and hospitals in Chekhov's universe—in such obvious correspondence between creator and creation there is no resonance of this additional drama. In Gissing's world the correspondence is something more obsessional, less clearly understood, more persistently presented, and charged always with resentment or the ostentation of despair. And hence to some critics he is a "whining" moralist rather than artist redeemed through creation. About his novels linger many intimations of their creator's mortality. As a novelist Gissing never transcended his turmoil and his misery.

No straightforward, honest or illuminating biography of Gissing exists. Those of his letters that have been published are obviously but a selection; and these selected letters are filled with surface preoccupations, and not with direct revelation of the inner man. It is in his fiction that we find Gissing both revealing and betraying himself. And it is to his fiction that we find

ourselves turning for a truer account of the man
himself. In doing this we must be clearly aware
that characters in novels are after all *fiction*. But
with Gissing it was only under this merciful veil
of *fiction* that he was ever able to break through
his reticent and evasive self and betray the
trouble and misery of his own heart. Again, to
quote Virginia Woolf, we approach such writers
as Gissing "through their lives as much as
through their works, and when we take up Gissing's letters, which have character but little wit
and no brilliance to illumine them, we feel that
we are filling in a design which we began to trace
out when we read *Demos* and *New Grub Street*
and *The Nether World.*"

If we knew nothing and could discover nothing
about the life of George Gissing and had only the
novels reputed to be by a man of that name, we
should presently be driven to invent a biography.
Why did he write long, remorseless, humourless
studies of the poor people in the slums of London
when obviously he hated all the circumstances
of their lives and in his heart seems to have hated
them too? One doesn't ask why Dickens wrote
about similar people—he liked them. Nor does
one question Zola's motive; so clearly his desire
was to be a "scientific" reformer. But why do
Gissing's young men experience consistently frustration or tragedy because they have no money
and can find no way of taking the places in so-

ciety that they believe their minds entitle them to take? And why Gissing's sentimental or vindictive treatment of women? Let us look first at the few facts of the man's life before we go on to seek further and more enlightening personal evidence from his books.

II

George Gissing was born in 1857 in the little town of Wakefield in northern England. He attended the grammar school there and because of precocious work was given a scholarship to study at Owens College, now the University of Manchester. After about three years in Owens College, Gissing left. He had involved himself in a difficulty that wrecked his academic career, and the reverberations of this experience were to torture him in guilt and humiliation throughout his life.

It is unfortunate that we have no more authentic account of Gissing's difficulties than that offered in Mr. Morley Roberts' *Private Life of Henry Maitland,* the book generally acknowledged to be a veiled biography of George Gissing. But when Mr. Roberts is dealing with the event which is so very important in any presentation of Gissing, we may assume that he would be most careful not to exaggerate the account either in the direction of exculpation or of censure. So it seems safe to accept his statement as a pretty

14

faithful record of the facts. This experience at Owens College offers a clue to much of the writer's work and to the man's behavior; and the account is here quoted in full:

"During that time in 1876, we students at Moorhampton College were much disturbed by a series of thefts in the common room, and from a locker room in which we kept our books and papers and our overcoats. Books disappeared unaccountably and so did coats. Money was taken from the pockets of coats left in the room, and nobody knew who was to blame for this. Naturally enough we suspected a porter or one of the lower staff, but we were wrong. Without our knowledge the college authorities set a detective to discover who was to blame. One day I went into the common room, and standing in front of the fire found a man, a young fellow about my age, called Sarle, with whom I frequently played chess—he was afterward president of the chess club at Oxford—and he said to me: 'Have you heard the news?' 'What news?' I asked. 'Your friend, Henry Maitland, has been stealing those things that we have lost,' he said. And when he said it I very nearly struck him, for it seemed a gross and incredible slander. But unfortunately it was true, and at that very moment Maitland was in gaol.'' *

That Gissing was caught in these petty pilfer-

* Pages 29 ff.

ings and that he served a sentence seem to be
unrefuted. And these further details, also taken
from Mr. Roberts' book, are offered straight-
forwardly here as explanatory of George Gissing.
The only possible interest these facts can have is
to help us account for that morbidity that dogged
his life, and out of which doubtless in large part
his fiction was destined to arise. The facts that
led up to this exposure and sentence are these:
the young man was lonely and he fell in love with
a girl with whom he had picked up an acquaintance. It is quite possible the story is true, that
to keep the girl off the streets he took this money
to buy her a sewing machine. When he had
served his sentence, friends, among them one or
two of his professors, helped him to get away to
America. He spent some time in Boston, then
he went on to Chicago, where he was driven to
supporting himself by writing fiction for the Sunday edition of the Chicago Tribune.

Much of this period of his life is to be found
recorded as the experience of the journalist
Whelpdale in *New Grub Street*. He was assisted
by a casual acquaintance in a restaurant to get
back to Europe. But before returning to England he spent some months in Germany. When
he did return to England he married the girl.
His domestic life was extremely unfortunate;
finally he was forced to live apart from this alco-
holic wife. After her death he married again.

It would seem that this girl was illiterate and bad tempered. From the evidence of his letters, this marriage was as hopeless as the first. Gissing explained to his friends who tried to dissuade him from this marriage that he was insufferably lonely. Most likely what one of the characters in *New Grub Street* says is what Gissing himself felt: "the time had come when he could not do without a wife. . . . Educated girls have a pronounced distaste for London garrets; not one in fifty thousand would share poverty with the brightest genius ever born . . . there is nothing to it but to look below one's level, and be grateful to the untaught woman who has pity on one's loneliness."

Gissing's latter days were spent with a French woman who had come to see him about translating *New Grub Street*. They lived in France, the last few months of his life in St. Jean de Luz, where Gissing died in 1904.

III

Most people are not made to feel the heavy hand of society. They are guided by common sense, prudence, luck, as you will. They may waken for a few moments from time to time to the realization that they are part of the conventional social pattern, and even if they are impelled to protest, their very habit of caution restrains them. But Gissing very early felt this

17

hand. With his youthful misstep he and society came into flagrant conflict. The penalty itself was severe enough, but the evil consequences to a man of Gissing's shrinking sensitiveness were much worse. It was with fear quiveringly upon him that Gissing found himself back in London, with the beast of Demos to be propitiated. It takes more courage than most young men have to defy what in their heart they fear. Shelley could do it, but Shelley had, along with the courage of his innate guilelessness, the security of birth and money. Gissing had neither birth—rather the profound consciousness of low birth—nor had he any money. He professed a great sympathy for the downtrodden. He felt himself to be one of them; and to raise the masses was in a sense to raise himself.

In a letter of 1880, Gissing wrote: "I mean to bring home to people the ghastly condition (material, mental, and moral) of our poor classes, to show the hideous injustice of our whole system of society, to give light upon the plan of altering it, and above all, to preach an enthusiasm for just and high *ideals* in this age of unmitigated egotism and 'shop.' I shall never write a book which does not keep all these ends in view." By such a "credo of realism" he tried to make himself believe that he loved the people. He wrote *Workers in the Dawn, The Nether World, Demos.* Yet as he grew older and gained security, he

18

dared to be more true to himself, he was more and more outspoken, until his final outburst of indignation in the *Ryecroft Papers*: "I am no friend of the people. As a force, by which the tenor of the time is conditioned, they inspire me with distrust, with fear; as a visible multitude, they make me shrink aloof, and often move me to abhorrence. For the greater part of my life, the people signified to me the London crowd, and no phrase of temperate meaning would utter my thoughts of them under that aspect. . . . Every instinct of my being is anti-democratic, and I dread to think of what our England may become when Demos rules irresistibly." This was in 1903. And again he writes in the same book: "The truth is that I have never learnt to regard myself as a 'member of society.' For me there have always been two entities—myself and the world—and the normal relation between these two has been hostile. Am I not still a lonely man, as far as ever from forming part of the social order? . . . And to think that at one time I called myself a socialist, a communist, anything you like of the revolutionary kind. Not for long, to be sure, and I suspect that there was always something in me that scoffed when my lips uttered such things."

Gissing's early fiction was a kind of propitiation to society; his middle work comes to be a form of revenge against society; when he is writing the books he loves most to write, he forgets society. And only then does he cease to express resentment or defiance through the stories of those young men of humble birth, good minds, but no money, who have been hurt by life—another name for established society; and who in their attempt to rise above their origins are monotonously frustrated by what appears to be an external obstacle. But this frustration, on closer observation, is clearly seen to result from some inner defect of character. Gissing himself seems only late in life to have been aware that the blame for his isolation did not belong to society alone, that he had brought his house down upon himself. And each time that there was a chance for Gissing to emerge from the self-imposed withdrawal from society, he would—as if fearing to be in the presence of people—forestall, by some such act as his second marriage, the attempts of friends to rescue him from his anguish and his despair. But he clung always to the conviction that he had been too severely punished. Decent society had flung him out and he had landed in the midst of the London herd. If he would exist he must make some concession, some adjustment to the social scheme. The one thing he could do to resolve his conflict, is just what he did: he took his own equipment and withdrew to record the scene. He was in this way less harassed by the crowd.

GEORGE GISSING

IV

When Gissing was twenty-five he published his first novel, *Workers in the Dawn* (1880). Mr. Austin Harrison (*Nineteenth Century,* September, 1906) points out that the hero, Arthur Golding, is a conscious autobiographical portrait of the author. This book is very hard to come by and for that reason the story is given here. And Miss May Yates in her admirable little book *George Gissing, An Appreciation,* says: "Arthur Golding is the first of those dubitative characters, rich in confessional interest, with whom Gissing is continually preoccupied. All the characters in this book reflect the inner discords and contemporary mental conflicts of the author."

Into Whitecross street on this Saturday night in which the book begins, comes Parson Edward Norman to visit his old friend Arthur Golding. He arrives in time to see Golding die. (Golding had robbed his employers, suffered the punishment for his crime, and had managed to kill himself with drink.) Parson Norman makes arrangements to call the next day for the little son, Arthur, about ten years old. He takes the child to the country to be brought up there with his daughter Helen. Arthur runs away and comes back to Whitecross Street, where he gets a job guiding the fake blind man. Then there is Michael Rumball the bird seller, and Ned Quirk the potato man. And while these are all obviously modeled after Dickens, they have their own peculiar power. If Dickens was wont to soften the lines, Gissing was not. These people are not in the slightest relieved by humor; they are stark and terrible when they are wicked; and they are, when they are good, not quite so wholly good as Dickens makes some of his people, and are therefore somewhat truer. Also, there are Mrs. Clinkseales and her daughter Lizzie; Mr. Tolladay, printer, who comes to be Arthur's kind employer, friend, and foster father. Helen Norman comes into the book later. There is Gilbert Gresham, Edward Norman's friend, and Maud, the daughter. Maud marries for money, lives abroad, and has a great many domestic battles, and finally shoots her husband. Orlando Whiffle is Norman's curate, very pedantic and very foolish. After the son has gone to the bad in a socially acceptable way, the young man keeps up appearances by becoming the lover of Maud. Under the tutelage and the sweet forbearance of Tolladay (a rather William Morris workshop hero), Arthur comes to be a good deal of a prig. But he studies painting with Gresham, an established artist, and Gresham comes to be very jealous of him. Into the plot at this moment is thrown the complicating factor of Pastor Norman's having made Gresham the guardian of Arthur Golding's legacy.

In all conventional novels, Arthur should have nearly married Maud Gresham, and finally married Helen Norman. But this is the sort of happy ending that filled Gissing with gloom. Temperamentally he couldn't have turned his novel in that way. Projecting his own misery upon the universe, Gissing was convinced that people were never happy, and so how could you give a novel a happy ending and expect it to be true? Helen, who now that her father is dead, is wealthy, leaves the Gresham's house to study in Germany. She is deeply interested in social service work, and this you feel is her way of hiding the fact that she loves Arthur. This Arthur senses, and as soon as he is convinced that it is true, and as soon also as he feels that perhaps he is in love with Helen, he perversely marries Carrie Mitchell. Carrie is illiterate, but pretty. She soon takes to drink and leaves Arthur. But periodically she returns to him. Either she comes herself, or Arthur receives calls from some of her friends who try to blackmail him. When Carrie discovers that the other "ladies of the house" are doing this, she comes and makes a rather fine statement to Arthur of her innocence. In one scene she tells him that she can't live with him again; that she isn't fit to live with him, and the implication is clear that it is because she has contracted a physical taint. All this part of the novel, which incidentally is presented with much

23

power of conviction, reminds one constantly of *Of Human Bondage;* of that scene chiefly where Philip Carey sees Mildred walking about the Piccadilly streets. Arthur gets a peculiar kind of inverted pleasure in confessing to Helen Norman that he is married, and in telling her the kind of woman Carrie is. Helen urges him to go out and bring Carrie back. Arthur goes out to look for Carrie and induce her to return. He thinks he sees her walking about Piccadilly. She doesn't come back. When Arthur sees the futility of his life, he migrates to the United States, and at Niagara Falls he makes the leap; lured or propelled by his own miseries he jumps into the maelstrom. The fact is very melodramatic, to be sure, but the portrayal of Arthur's mental state preceding the event, the cumulative effect of the analysis of Arthur, makes the conclusion of the book more moving than one would expect.

Probably the most interesting and yet the most false part of the novel is Chapter XIV, called *Mind Growth,* in which Gissing appears to publish the diary that Helen Norman has kept during her stay in Germany. It is filled, first, with literary and historical allusions; with considerations of problems of philosophy and of sociology and politics. It is Gissing himself, more than Helen Norman. It sounds absurd to read it for a portrayal of Helen, so obviously is it Gissing's own. All the while it sets up this irritating incongruity, and ends in blurring the impression of Helen. And yet this is very characteristic. In much of his work he seems to identify himself with some one of the women in his books. Mr. Seccombe says of him: "The distinctive qualities of Gissing at the time of his setting forth were a scholarly style, rather fastidious and academic in its restraint, and the personal discontent, slightly morbid, of a self-conscious student who finds himself in the position of a sensitive woman in a crowd."

V

Gissing spent the greater part of his time thinking about himself. In his novels when he is supposedly writing about other people, he is really writing his own history. This mechanism is made clear in a letter from Schopenhauer to Goethe, dated November 11, 1815: "Every work has its origin in a happy thought, and the latter gives the joy of conception; the birth, however, the carrying out, is, in my own case at least, not without pain; for then I stand before my own soul, like an inexorable judge before a prisoner lying on the rack, and make it answer until there is nothing left to ask. Almost all the errors and unutterable follies of which doctrines and philosophies are so full seem to me to spring from a lack of this probity. The truth was not found, not because it was unsought, but because the in-

tention always was to find again instead some
preconceived opinion or other, or at least not to
wound some favourite idea, and with that aim in
view subterfuges had to be employed against
both other people and the thinker himself. It is
the courage of making a clean breast of it in face
of every question that makes the philosopher. He
must be like Sophocles' Oedipus, who, seeking enlightenment concerning his terrible fate, pursues
his indefatigable enquiry, even when he divines
that appalling horror awaits him in the answer.
But most of us carry in our hearts the Jocasta,
who begs Oedipus for God's sake not to enquire
further; and we give way to her and that is the
reason why philosophy stands where it does.''

This is the reason not only why philosophy
stands where it does, but the reason, moreover,
why in Gissing's novels, though perpetually absorbed with Gissing's own conflicts, there is never
probity, clarification and release.

We shall turn now to one of Gissing's earliest
novels, *Isabel Clarendon,* and we shall assume a
close correspondence between the young author
and Bernard Kingcote, the hero. The theme is
one that Gissing used very often. Gissing was
twenty-nine when he wrote this book; the hero is
about the same age. The outline of the story follows—again given here because of the scarcity of
the book:

Bernard Kingcote, with a small fund, retires

from London's hard commercial life to the country. There he meets a scholar clergyman and his wife. The two men find their chief delight in making careful textual readings in Shakespeare. The great lady of the countryside is Isabel Clarendon, an attractive and well-to-do widow. In her home is Ada Warren, illegitimate daughter of Mr. Clarendon, who spends most of her days in the library. Ada is clever, intellectually rather precocious; she is also morose and crotchety. Bernard Kingcote meets these people. He convinces himself he is in love with Isabel. He is both attracted and repelled by Isabel's wealth and social position. Isabel really seems to be in love with Bernard; eventually she is really in love with him. At the moment when there is a possibility of Bernard and Isabel finding a life of happiness together, the worthless husband of Kingcote's sister dies, leaving the sister destitute. Bernard listens to the Jocasta in his heart. He seems actually glad of his escape from Isabel. He goes to London to live with his sister Mary. Isabel tries to get him back, but, buoyed up by his formal puritanical conscience, he resists. He enjoys his own nobility and his suffering. And Isabel marries a man she has known and respected for years. The story ends with a final interview between Bernard and Isabel, in which with dignity and with passion she pleads with him not to be afraid of his love for her. He seems still to believe that he loves her; but he finds it difficult to convince himself. He gives her up and goes back to his sister in Camden Town.

In the book there is considerable narrative power; the form of the novel is well managed. At the same time, there is a stilted, sophomoric quality, especially in the obviously "literary," monotonous sentences. All the external scenery seems very trumped up—the garden at night, the nightingale singing. Worse than this, the people remain, for the most part, paper people. It is true that at moments, they come to life, as for example Kingcote pacing the London streets, fighting with his own evil fate; Isabel, ill, sending for and receiving Kingcote; and much of the talk and behaviour of Ada Warren. But these are only sporadic resurrections of a group of people that might, by a writer of greater fictional power, have been infused with the life of inner necessity.

This book makes quite clear the besetting sin of Gissing: he is absurdly glorifying woman, making himself as a writer quite sentimentally ridiculous, and so, one feels, protesting too much sentimental Victorian masculinity—obviously because he did not actually possess it: or belittling woman in a bitter and vindictive and ferocious way that even the worst of his women seems not to deserve. As might be expected, the best parts of this novel are those which deal with the brother and sister working out their lives in Camden

Town, because these are the victimized people that Gissing can most sympathetically identify himself with. One feels convinced that Kingcote could have married Isabel, got a job, and supported his sister Mary from a distance.

But Gissing imposes his own frustrations upon his hero. He loved the crucifixion. Withdrawing thus from Isabel, and seeking refuge in his life with his sister Mary, Kingcote evaded the necessity of living up to the demands of a husband to one of Isabel's social class. And there is a definite kind of Gissing pride revealed; it was easier for Kingcote to live with a sister he was supporting than to feel he was marrying "a lady with money."

Isabel Clarendon (1886) is generally admitted to be the most autobiographical of all his books. The novel is further enlightening because it contains rather full delineations of the hero's parents, likenesses which seem to be drawn from Gissing's father and mother.

Let this description, then, of Mr. Kingcote, stand for Gissing's father. He was "not a man of strong character, though he possessed considerable ability in various directions; his temperament was impulsive, imaginative, affectionate; he was wholly ruled by his wife . . . the children appeared to stand apart from their parents; to be thrown very much upon their own resources. . . . Mrs. Kingcote [let her stand for Gissing's mother], though behaving to them with all motherly care, did not win their love, neither appeared to miss it." For Mrs. Kingcote, external facts of life sufficed—details of housekeeping. In the story, she had run off and married, chiefly it would appear to have a house of her own to rule and regulate.

There are a few quotations from the novel bearing upon Bernard Kingcote himself that are worth giving. "In Kingcote there existed his father's intellectual and emotional qualities, together with a certain stiffness of moral attitude derived from his mother. His prejudices were intense, their character being determined by the refinement and idealism of his nature. An enemy would have called him offensively aristocratic; only malicious ignorance could have accused him of snobbishness." "His was an essentially feminine nature." "Few men surpassed Bernard Kingcote in ingenious refinement of self-torture." His "was not the face of a man at ease with his own heart, or with the circumstances amid which his life had fallen." He wanted to be free: "from sights and sounds which disgust me, from the contiguity of mean and hateful people, from suggestions which make life hideous; free to live with my fancies, and in the thoughts of men I love." "One ambition there is which has ruled my life: a high one. I have wished to win a woman's love."

GEORGE GISSING

The early parts of the novel *Born in Exile* are probably the most autobiographical passages to be found in Gissing's work. The later life of the hero, Godwin Peak, departs in its outer aspects from Gissing's, but the spirit and tone are very similar. There is a very fine chapter in the novel which tells how an uncle opens "Peak's Dining and Refreshment Rooms" directly opposite the college where his nephew was a student. To Godwin this blatant and insensitive advertising of their relation to trade is a bitter humiliation, and he leaves college because he is unable to endure the constant reminder of his humble origins. Godwin is a gifted and promising student. His shame and morbid pride permit the restaurant to wreck his academic career—just as Gissing's career was wrecked by the shameful episode of the theft. Godwin proceeds to London and works at journalism. Then he meets the daughter of one of his old professors, and with a desire to win this girl, he violates all his intellectual convictions and enters upon a career in the ministry. He believes that to be ordained will increase his social stature and thus he will be able to marry the girl. His religious and social hypocrisies are exposed, and he loses himself in the whirlpool of London life, more than ever an exile and an alien.

VI

Gissing's treatment of women in his novels is most revealing of his own character. In *Thyrza* there is a sentimental idealization of a marriage, and one finds it almost necessary to believe that this is a re-telling of the facts of his own first marriage, idealized to happiness. Of the character Elgar, in *The Emancipated,* Gissing says: Elgar "couldn't read the marriage column in a newspaper without feeling a distinct jealousy of all the male creatures there mentioned." Yet later in the same book we find the following, which is just as truly Gissing: "How many wives and husbands love each other? Not one pair in five thousand. In the average pair . . . there is not only mutual criticism, but something even of mutual dislike. That makes love impossible. Habit takes its place."

Gissing is not Dostoevsky, and clouded as Gissing was by his romantic, sentimental attitude towards women, he could never see life with the realistic clarity of Dostoevsky and know how inextricably hatred and love are bound together. Gissing had read Dostoevsky and he might have gained something of the Russian writer's vision of love, if he had not been so penitentially involved himself in love adventures. As an incorrigible romantic Gissing loved to build both castles and dungeons in Spain—each in its way caricaturing reality. Yet it was characteristic of him at the same time to view his "dungeons" as true and to despise the other romantics who wrote precisely as he did. In his novel, *The Odd Women,* he has Rhoda Nun say, writing his own death warrant: "If every novelist could be strangled and thrown into the sea, we should have some chance of reforming women. The girl's nature was corrupted with sentimentality, like that of all but every woman who is intelligent enough to read what is called the best fiction, but not intelligent enough to understand its vice. Love—love—love; a sickening sameness of vulgarity. What is more vulgar than the ideal of novelists? They won't represent the actual world; it would be too dull for their readers. In real life, how many men and women *fall in love?* Not one in every ten thousand, I am convinced. Not one married pair in ten thousand have felt for each other as two or three couples do in *every* novel. There is the sexual instinct, of course, but that is quite a different thing; the novelists daren't talk about that. The paltry creatures daren't tell the one truth that would be profitable. The result is that women imagine themselves noble and glorious when they are most near the animals."

VII

As a novelist, Gissing never came to terms with himself. Though always turning inward he was like a squirrel in a cage, doing dizzy circles around himself as futile gymnastics of escape. The growth and development of George Meredith, brilliantly suggested by André Maurois in his *Aspects of Biography,* was not possible for George Gissing. M. Maurois says that Meredith was a snob, and he wrote *Evan Harrington* and overcame his snobbishness; he was an egoist, and he wrote *The Egoist* and conquered that vice, and so on. If this is true at all of Gissing, it is only very slightly true; for by temperament and early conditioning, Gissing seems to have been a man of much greater rifts in character than Meredith, and of much less decisive will.

It was in the cloistered life of the scholar that he would have known greater happiness; there he would have found the best occasion for his gifts. His humiliation at college and the subsequent scar that he bore throughout his life closed to him the possibility of any such career. And yet he knew many modern languages — German, Spanish, Italian, French—and he had for Greek and Latin and archeology a passion that, given a chance, would have carried him far. His fiction was to him an irritation, something to be done that he might not starve. To escape this irritation, he studied constantly, especially history, and when finally the leisure did come, he wrote books nearer to his keenest desire: *By the Ionian Sea, The Ryecroft Papers, Veranilda.* Moreover if it had not

34

been for a ferocious and damaging pride, Gissing would have been helped to work that he loved by friends and acquaintances who appreciated his splendid equipment for scholarship. But he was cursed not only with this pride, but with domestic miseries; and these, with his shrinking sensitiveness and his raw social wounds that sent him deeper and deeper into retirement, made inevitable the life he lived.

He read and dreamed himself into the past, and the result of this faithful and illuminated dreaming is to be found in *Veranilda.* When he visited southern Italy, he was himself something of a spirit of a vanished age, and he was very happy in that brief experience. He confesses: "Every man has his intellectual desire; mine is to escape life as I know it and dream myself into that old world which was the imaginative delight of my boyhood." And it is true that all through Gissing's life of turmoil, ill-health, and despair, he was able by the power of this imaginative daydreaming, by his love of history and the classics, to find a little repose.

A year or two before he died he wrote, in *The Ryecroft Papers:*

For of myself it might be said that whatever folly is possible to a moneyless man, that folly I have at one time or another committed. Within my nature there seemed to be no faculty of rational self-guidance. Boy and man, I blundered into every ditch and bog which lay within sight of my way. Never did silly mortal reap such harvest of experience; never had anyone so many bruises to show for it. Thwack, thwack! No sooner had I recovered from one sound drubbing than I put myself in the way of another. "Unpractical" I was called by those who spoke mildly; "idiot"—I am sure—by many a ruder tongue. And idiot I see myself, whenever I glance back over the long, devious road. Something, obviously, I lacked from the beginning, some balancing principle granted to most men in one or another degree. I had brains, but they were no help to me in the common circumstances of life.

It is all true, but even here the Jocasta in his heart is not silent—the self-indulging pleasure principle which is the Jocasta of us all. Gissing is luxuriating in the spectacle of his failure. He told the truth, but it never made him free.

CHAPTER II

TIME PASSES

Of Human Bondage, by Somerset Maugham
The Old Wives' Tale, by Arnold Bennett
Buddenbrooks, by Thomas Mann

CERTAIN novels, we said in discussing Gissing, seem so completely detached from their authors that few traces of the relation between the creator and his work remain to tease our curiosity and make us half-glimpse a psychological drama. If they had their inception in the maladjustments, the unresolved conflicts, the unfulfilled dreams, of their author, these have been so effectively projected and dramatized that they live their own rounded and independent life. Such a dramatic novel as *Pride and Prejudice,* or such a serene birth-to-death chronicle as *The Old Wives' Tale,* has this autonomous air. Who stops his reading to wonder uneasily about its author, as one wonders about the author of *Sons and Lovers* or of *Crime and Punishment*? What has been called the chronicle novel is perhaps more likely to present this effect of detachment than the dramatic novel. The author's effort to resist absorption in this or that intense individual experience, to stand apart and watch the stream of life flow past for a long period of years, must tend to create in him a mood impersonal and contemplative. The ability to achieve and sustain

this mood is in itself evidence of at least temporary balance, adjustment and release. It would
seem that a chronicle novel could scarcely be
written except in this mood, and that one way of
evoking the mood is to apprehend time as itself
the leading character in the human story. In the
chronicle, as Edwin Muir puts it, time is external;
"it flows past the beholder; it flows over and
through the figures he evokes. Instead of nar-
rowing to a point, the point fixed by passion or
fear or fate in the dramatic novel, it stretches
away indefinitely, running with a scarcely per-
ceptible check over all the barriers that might
have marked its end."

In the case of dramatic novels, the tendency of
the reader is to become deeply involved in the
conflict; to identify himself with the Paul of *Sons
and Lovers,* or with *Ivan Karamazov, or Mary
Olivier.* When the tension is relaxed, the conflict resolved, and the arena vacant, he reassumes
his own personality and comes back into his waking life as from a vivid dream. But the effect
of such novels as *War and Peace, Buddenbrooks,*
and *The Forsyte Saga* is usually quite different.
As the years slip by in these books and one generation insensibly replaces another, we are gradually detached from individual lives and left in
contemplation of life, flowing through and past
the generations. "This cosmic progression," to
quote Edwin Muir once more, "gives a different

value to all the particular happenings, making the tragic pathetic, the inevitable accidental, the final relative.'' Our mood becomes meditative, elegiac. We are tranquilized by a process quite different from the catharsis of the dramatic experience, and left brooding, not over the significance of this or that individual destiny, but over the meaning of the whole human adventure.

This effect is not, one imagines, easy for the artist to achieve. To chronicle events through the years may result in a meaningless catalogue. The individual must lose some of his significance in the long perspective; but there is danger that life, too, may come to seem trivial. The question of form is a less sharply defined problem than in the dramatic novel, where it grows out of the conflict, and where the novelist's task is to show how the conflict came about, what forces are involved, what complications develop, and how it is at last resolved, in destruction or reconciliation. In contrast with such a strict and logical progression, we have in the chronicle a ''loose concatenation of episodes,'' bound together only by the conception of time. How can we be given the satisfaction that comes from the shaping of events, the tracing of cause and effect relationships, the movement to a climax, and the falling away into a solution? There must be a design if we are to be left tranquil and satisfied, not weary and confused. How Tolstoy deals with

41

the problem in *War and Peace* has been made the subject of illuminating analysis by several critics —notably Percy Lubbock. That is the supreme example of the chronicle novel. But other novels less great give the same kind of pleasure and are worth study.

II

Somerset Maugham's *Of Human Bondage* is no family chronicle, no slow birth to death progression. Its very title suggests an emotional involvement, a struggle for escape, that promises a dramatic development. Fill out the title from Spinoza's *Ethics*—"Of Human Bondage, or the Strength of the Emotions"—and one is prepared for a plunge into some intense form of human experience. And one takes it, too; such a deep plunge that there are probably few characters in modern English fiction with whom readers more readily identify themselves than with Philip Carey.* But for all that, there are qualities in the novel—to be noted presently—that leave one at the end in a mood very different from that in which, for example, a Dostoevsky novel leaves us, though Philip's emotional entanglements are almost Russian.

The most lasting bondage in which Philip is held is that of his own temperament, and his tem-

* A guess, of course, but based on comments from many students.

perament is determined largely by the accident of his deformity—a club foot. Thinking over his life towards the end of the book, he realizes how this deformity has warped his character, and yet how it had developed in him a power of introspection that has given him as much delight as misery. One of the pitfalls of his nature is self-pity. A little boy, just after his mother's death, he weeps, yet keenly enjoys the sensation he is causing among some sympathetic ladies by his sorrow, and wishes he could stay longer with them to be made much of. Awakened to acute self-consciousness by the brutality with which he is treated by curious boys in the school dormitory, his school life becomes one of intermittent torment. He soon learns that when anyone becomes angry with him for any reason, some reference will be made to his foot. He finds himself doing odd bits of playing to the gallery, to excite compassion; as when a schoolmate accidentally breaks a penholder belonging to Philip, and Philip, with tears, declares it was given to him by his mother before she died—though he knows he had bought it a few weeks before. "He did not know in the least what had made him invent that pathetic story, but he was quite as unhappy as though it had been true." The habit continues even after he has learned to understand it, and he lapses into it whenever he is weakened by suffering. When Mildred is irritated by his persistent love on one occasion, "he hesitated a moment, for he had an instinct that he could say something that would move her. It made him almost sick to utter the words,"—but he utters them nevertheless—" 'You don't know what it is to be a cripple. Of course you don't like me. I can't expect you to.' He was beginning to act now, and his voice was husky and low." And she softens at the pathos.

He develops ways of escape and defense: reading, first, in his uncle's queerly assorted library, where he forgot the life around him and formed "the most delightful habit in the world—reading. He did not know that he was thus providing himself with a refuge from all the distress of life; he did not know either that he was creating for himself an unreal world which would make the real world of every day a source of bitter disappointment." The wide knowledge gained from his books made him contemptuous of his companions' stupidity, and he found he had a knack in saying bitter things, "which caught people on the raw." Thus he could defend himself, but he couldn't make himself popular, and he longed for easy intercourse with his schoolmates, and would gladly have changed places with the dullest boy in the school who was whole of limb. He develops a cool ironic manner; he evens learns to control his sensitive blushing; he can protect himself, but he is still in bondage. When the physician at the hospital where he is studying asks Philip casually to display his foot, to compare it with that of the patient under examination in the clinic, Philip forced himself to appear indifferent, allowed the students to look at the foot as long as they wished—"when you've quite done," said Philip with an ironical smile. . . . "And felt how jolly it would be to jab a chisel into their necks." He becomes an adept in self-analysis—"a vice as subtle as drug-taking."

What Philip suffers from his deformed foot is mild compared with the misery he undergoes when he falls in love with Mildred. It is an emotion so different from anything he has ever dreamed or read about—this aching of the soul, this painful yearning—that he is profoundly shocked when he is forced to identify it as love. Mildred, with her insolent pale thin mouth and anæmic skin, has been described somewhere as an implacable pale green worm who crawls through the book. The very fact that Philip is blinded by no illusions about her, that he sees how unhealthy, commonplace, odiously genteel, vulgar and selfish she is, convinces us that the passion is irresistible. Lovers of unworthy objects in fiction are usually clearly deluded; we, the readers, see that, and look for the waning of the passion with the discovery of the truth. But Philip knows the truth from the beginning, and we agonize with him over this divorce between reason and

45

emotion, this split in consciousness where the reason watches, disgusted, repelled, estimating the passion at its true value, but unable to affect the emotions, which go their own lamentable way. "His reason was someone looking on, observing the facts, but powerless to interfere; it was like those gods of Epicurus, who saw the doings of men from their empyrean heights and had no might to alter one smallest particle of what occurred." There are moments when he loathes Mildred, moments again when he feels noble because of the sacrifices he makes for her, other moments—like the blessed pauses in an illness—when the temperature falls and he thinks he is released. Once when she treats him with an insolence that humiliates him, "he looked at her neck and thought how he would like to jab it with the knife he had for his muffin. He knew enough anatomy to make pretty certain of getting the carotid artery. And at the same time he wanted to cover her thin pale face with kisses." He tastes the depths of voluptuous self-torture when he gives Mildred and Griffiths—his friend for whom the apparently passionless Mildred has a violent infatuation—money to go off together on a week-end trip. He is sick with anguish when he makes the offer, yet "the torture of it gave him a strange subtle sensation." The devil of self-torture always lurks in him. There is a strange sequel when he later takes Mildred and her baby into his little flat and supports them, though he no longer has any desire for Mildred. This physical indifference so piques Mildred that she throws herself at his head, and rejected, takes a vicious revenge by utterly destroying all the furnishings of the apartment, even slashing Philip's few paintings, relics of his art studies. But even that is not the end of Mildred; she comes back again and again, with each reappearance more degraded. When she is finally lost, Philip sometimes wandered through the streets haunted by prostitutes, wishing and dreading to see her, catching a glimpse of someone resembling her that gave him a sharp stab of hope or of sickening dismay—he scarcely knew which. Relieved when it was not she, he was yet disappointed and seized with horror of himself. "Would he never be free from that passion? At the bottom of his heart, notwithstanding everything, he felt that a strange desperate thirst for that vile woman would always linger. That love had caused him so much suffering that he knew he would never, never be quite free of it. Only death could finally assuage his desire." There are times in the course of this strange passion when Philip could step over into Dostoevsky's world and feel at ease with the most accomplished masochist of them all.

Compelling as is the drama of Philip's struggle, it is to other aspects of the novel that the final impression is due. There is the sense of change, of relentless moving on, that marks the chronicle, though the space of years actually covered in *Of Human Bondage* is not great—perhaps twenty-five or thirty. Philip moving from one group to another, in his restless search for adjustment, loses sight of this or that person for a time; then sees him again, changed, older. There are his clergyman uncle and his aunt, middle-aged when they take the orphaned nephew into their home, growing into old age, dying; there is Hayward, fascinating and brilliant in the eyes of twenty-year-old Philip, gradually revealing himself as Philip grows more astute to be a shallow poseur, whose mind grows more and more flabby and his charm more and more tarnished. There is Cronshaw, the poet of the Montparnasse cafés, center of a little circle of the initiated; leading an ever shabbier and more sordid life, coming to die wretchedly in London. And Mildred herself, who runs rapidly through the stages that take her from a curiously attractive waitress in an ABC teashop to a diseased prostitute haunting Piccadilly. It is Philip's reflective attitude towards all these mutations that helps to create the effect of philosophic detachment characteristic of the chronicle novel.

Then Philip's career is so varied and experimental that he seems to have led several lives. And there is such richness of detail in the account of his art studies in Paris, his medical training in London hospitals, his dismal interlude as a shop clerk; there are so many people in each little universe whose lives Philip observes with the same sort of interested detachment with which Maugham himself observes Philip,—that we feel we are watching the unrolling of an elaborate panorama. There is not the rigid selection of detail that in the dramatic novel makes everything bear directly on the main conflict. For the interest is not so much in the final resolution of the conflict as in Philip's arrival at a comprehension of its nature and its place in some general scheme of human existence. He begins quite early seeking consciously to understand the meaning of life, as well as to make his own difficult adjustments to it. Often this intellectual need—stimulated by his emotional difficulties—is more pressing than a decision about his career or an escape from the degrading bondage to the unspeakable Mildred. The reader begins presently to share Philip's philosophic concern with what life is all about.

It is towards the chapter that follows "Of Human Bondage" in Spinoza's *Ethics* that the novel is moving, though one can scarcely say that it arrives—"Of Human Freedom, or the Control of the Understanding." From time to time Philip feels that he understands himself and life and can control both. When he talks with Cron-

shaw in Paris, he is challenged to say what he
really thinks he is in the world for, and he an-
swers vaguely—to do one's duty, to make the best
use of one's faculties, and to avoid hurting other
people. This he calls abstract morality, and he is
indignant with Cronshaw for ridiculing his weak
reasoning, and for setting up a thoroughly self-
centered philosophy—that men seek but one thing
in life, their pleasure. Philip had always believed conventionally in duty and goodness. As
he goes on through his own difficult experiences,
and especially as he watches day after day the
procession of humanity through the clinic of the
hospital, he comes to see only facts. The impression was "neither of tragedy nor of comedy. . . .
It was manifold and various; there were tears
and laughter, happiness and woe; it was tedious
and interesting and indifferent; it was as you
saw it; it was tumultuous and passionate; it was
grave; it was sad and comic; it was trivial; it
was simple and complex; joy was there and despair; the love of mothers for their children, and
of men for women; lust trailed itself through the
rooms with leaden feet, punishing the guilty and
the innocent, helpless wives and wretched children; drink seized men and women and cost its
inevitable price; death sighed in these rooms and
the beginning of life, filling some poor girl with
terror and shame, was diagnosed there. There

was neither good nor bad there. There were just facts. It was life.''

So Philip cultivated a disdain for idealism, which he had found meant for the most part a cowardly shrinking from life. But meeting a man with a passion for Spain and particularly for the painting of El Greco, Philip began to divine something new, to feel on the brink of a discovery, a new kind of realism in which facts ''were transformed by the more vivid light in which they were seen.'' There was some mysterious significance in these paintings, but the tongue in which the message came was unknown to him. ''He saw what looked like the truth as by flashes of lightning on a dark stormy night you might see a mountain range. He seemed to see that a man need not leave his life to chance, but that his will was powerful; he seemed to see that self-control might be as passionate and as active as the surrender to passion; he seemed to see that the inward life might be as manifold, as varied, as rich with experience as the life of one who conquered realms and explored unknown lands.''

These remain but flashes. He finds most satisfaction in the conviction that life has no meaning. ''Life was insignificant and death without consequence.'' He exulted as he had in his boyhood when the weight of a belief in God was lifted from his shoulders. He felt free. ''If life was

meaningless, the world was robbed of its cruelty."
But Cronshaw had once given him a little Per-
sian rug, and told him that the meaning of life
was hidden in its pattern; and now he thinks he
discerns it. "As the weaver elaborated his pattern for no need but the pleasure of his æsthetic
sense, so might a man live his life, or if one was
forced to believe that his actions were outside his
choosing, so might a man look at his life, that it
made a pattern. . . . Out of the manifold events
of his life, his deeds, his feelings, his thoughts, he
might make a design, regular, elaborate, complicated, or beautiful; and though it might be no
more than an illusion that he had the power of
selection, though it might be no more than a fantastic legerdemain in which appearances were
interwoven with moonbeams, that did not matter:
it seemed, and so to him it was. . . . There was
one pattern, the most obvious, perfect, and beautiful, in which a man was born, grew to man-
hood, married, produced children, toiled for his
bread, and died; but there were others, intricate
and wonderful, in which happiness did not enter
and in which success was not attempted; and in
them might be discovered a more troubling
grace." Philip felt he was casting aside the last
of his illusions in throwing over the desire for
happiness. Measured by that desire, his life was
horrible, but it might be measured by something
else. Happiness and pain were details in the

elaboration of the design. Anything that happened to him henceforth would simply be one more motive to add to the complexity of the pattern. When the end came and it was completed, he would find it none the less beautiful because he alone knew of its existence and "with his death it would cease to be."

Philip's final acceptance of the most obvious pattern is brought about by his meeting with Sally, a girl with a very simple pagan attitude towards living, as radiantly healthy as Mildred was sickly, as tranquil as Philip is restless, as soothingly maternal as any man could wish his ideal woman to be—yet not as convincing as the dreadful Mildred, who seems the reality, whereas Sally is one of the dreams belonging to the Golden Age. Freedom to Philip suddenly takes on the aspect of lonely voyaging over a waste of waters; a quiet home with Sally is a fair harbor. "He thought of his desire to make a design, intricate and beautiful, out of the myriad, meaningless facts of life: had he not seen also that the simplest pattern, that in which a man was born, worked, married, had children, and died, was likewise the most perfect? It might be that to surrender to happiness was to accept defeat, but it was a defeat better than many victories."

II

There is nothing more obvious than the fact

that all old people were once young. Here is the simplest aspect of the part played by time in our lives. But every now and then a commonplace like this strikes upon a sensitive imagination like a revelation and induces a profound emotion out of which grows a work of art. This happened to Arnold Bennett one evening in 1903, when he was dining in a restaurant in Paris, and an old woman, laden with parcels, came in, looking so fat, clumsy and grotesque that everyone laughed. "I reflected," writes Mr. Bennett, "that this woman was once young, slim, perhaps beautiful —certainly free from these ridiculous mannerisms. Her case is a tragedy. One ought to be able to make a heart-rending novel out of the case of such a woman as she. Every stout aging woman is not grotesque—far from it; but there is an extreme pathos in the mere fact that every stout aging woman was once a young girl with the unique charm of youth in her form and movements and in her mind. And the fact that the change from the young girl to the stout aging woman is made up of an infinite number of infinitesimal changes, each unperceived by her, only adds to the pathos. It was at that instant that I was visited by the idea of writing the book which ultimately became *The Old Wives' Tale*." De Maupassant's *Une Vie* had recorded the life of a woman from girlhood to old age, with the average experiences of young love, marriage, motherhood, sorrow, loss, and disillusionment; and this novel Bennett admired so much that he determined to create its English counterpart. But with characteristic assurance, he wished to go De Maupassant one better, and to write, not of one woman, but of two.

He placed his two heroines, Constance and Sophia Baines, in the midst of the Victorian era and in the heart of the provincial district in England which he knew most intimately. He had grown up in one of the Five Towns in Staffordshire, where is made all the everyday crockery used in the United Kingdom; and had passed his own childhood in the house in St. Luke's Square where the Baines family lived, next to their draper's establishment. The county is in the center of England, the Five Towns in the center of the county, and St. Luke's Square in the center of the oldest of the Five Towns. It is all as English, all as average as possible—a life "unsung by searchers after the extreme." Bennett had withdrawn from it soon enough—he was twenty-one when he went to London—to be enabled to view it in perspective. With a strong sense of its humorous aspects and its limitations, yet deeply in sympathy with it, he gives a convincing representation of its intimate daily life and a moving interpretation of its people. These are the men and women who stay on Main Street; here are Mid-Victorian parlors, Nottingham lace curtains, kitchens, sulky servants, afternoon teas, children's parties, pampered fox-terriers, local fairs and local scandals, marketing and church-going—the whole world of the commonplace and the everyday.

Sophia and Constance, delightful girls at the outset of the tale, grow up in this little world of the Five Towns, fundamentally alike in the sterling traits of character belonging to the Baines stock, but different enough to seek different stages on which to play their parts. Constance, the more pliable and conventional, marries the head clerk of her father's shop, remains in the house in St. Luke's Square, and retraces almost every design in her mother's life, as housekeeper, wife and mother. Sophia, more rebellious and spirited, elopes to Paris with the attractive, irresponsible Gerald Scales, lives through some ecstasies and many bitter disillusionments, cuts herself off completely for thirty years from the Five Towns, adapts herself to Paris life after her worthless husband disappears, and becomes the successful manager of a most exemplary pension. First we follow the story of Constance through the years up to the point where her grown son leaves her to study art in London. Then we go back and pick up the thread of Sophia's life, follow it through the same span of years, until an illness and the accidental renewal of contact with the Five Towns lead her to rejoin her sister in St.

Luke's Square. The currents of their lives then flow in one stream to the end.

Sophia's life had more spectacular possibilities. One might have expected her to develop traits very different from those of her home-keeping sister. But throughout all her French experience, there persist in Sophia the characteristic Five Towns virtues and limitations. Sophia is as impermeable to Paris as Strether in *The Ambassadors* is vulnerable. She learns to speak its language and to play the game of making a living according to its rules, and to manage its people in the service of her ends. On the common ground of thrift, she and its tradesmen can meet in understanding and sympathy. But the beauty of Paris, its art, its atmosphere, its sense of the value of the passing moment, the many graces of its living, all these have no voice for her spirit. She is captivated during the brief days of her happiness with Gerald by the gaiety and glitter of the café life. But she is soon aware of the hollowness of that. And later she sees the underside of the lives of the prostitutes on Montmartre, and condemns such living—not so much for its immorality as for its laxity and its untidiness and its ultimate failure. Not "What a sinner!" but "What a fool!" she thinks of the woman who had nursed her in her illness; "if I couldn't have made a better courtesan than this miserable woman, I should have drowned myself." It was the Five Towns instinct for good workmanship cropping up.

Once only does Paris almost win out over the Five Towns. This is during Sophia's little holiday dinner with Chirac, the journalist, who in many of her most difficult experiences had come to her assistance with delicate consideration. The atmosphere of the tiny restaurant is agreeable, reassuring, friendly; Chirac's love-making is not unexpected. Curiosity not merely about him but about herself had tempted Sophia tacitly to encourage him. She is close to that experimental attitude towards life that had amazed her some years before in Chirac—when he had gone to see a guillotining as a psychological experience, "to observe himself in such circumstances." "How strange even nice Frenchmen are," she had thought. Now she herself is almost on the edge of experimentation. But from some obscure instinct she repulses him. Mr. Bennett, with that rather hard unshaded certainty of his, which is in such great contrast to Conrad's tentativeness in the face of the psychological problem, explains her refusal as the result of a certain haughty moral independence, leading her to despise any open expression of emotion—a Baines trait, a Five Towns trait. Chirac suffered too openly. If ever there was a chance for Sophia to flower into graciousness and become sensitive to other than Five Towns values in life, it was at this moment. The danger was that she would close her doors against enriching experience and grow harder, narrower, more barren. And she does. She becomes the landlady—efficient, stylish, diplomatic, armed against every trickery, who could not be startled and could not be swindled. After thirty years in Paris, all that she brings back to St. Luke's Place—aside from a skill in dressing that no one in the Five Towns possessed —is the French poodle, Fossette.

After the funeral of Constance, who outlives her sister, no one is left in the house but the cook and the infirm French poodle, Fossette—"sole relic of the connection between the Baines family and Paris." The tearful servant prepared the dog's dinner and placed it before her in the customary soup-plate in the customary corner. Fossette sniffed at it and then walked away and lay down with a sigh in front of the kitchen fire. She had been deranged in her habits that day and was conscious of neglect due to events that passed her comprehension. "However after a few minutes she began to reconsider the matter. She glanced at the soup-plate, and, on the chance that it might after all contain something worth inspection, she awkwardly balanced herself on her old legs, and went to it again."

So the curtain falls on the *Old Wives' Tale*. It contains many episodes that, if isolated on their little stage, would furnish the material of a dramatic novel.

There is the murder committed by a relative of the Baines family, a tragedy that might well be the climax of a dramatic novel. But it is important in the story simply because Constance's husband, Samuel, embraced his unfortunate cousin's cause, wore himself out in the effort to save him from the gallows, lost the fight, and died of exhaustion and disappointment. The story flows on past this tragedy. More significant still in creating the final effect of the *Old Wives' Tale* is the handling of the siege of Paris in 1870. Sophia is in Paris during the siege, struggling to draw together the broken threads of her life after her illness and the desertion of Gerald. With the business sense that is her Five Towns inheritance, she has managed to secure lodgers, provide them with food, and find a modest profit in it. "For Sophia the conclusion of the siege meant chiefly that prices went down. . . . The signing of the treaty reduced the value of Sophia's two remaining hams from about five pounds apiece to the usual price of hams." Bennett had acquired this sense of what the siege meant to ordinary people by questioning an old French servant about his experiences at the time: "You went through the Siege of Paris, didn't you?" he asked. The old man turned uncertainly to his wife: "The Siege of Paris? Yes, we did, didn't we?'' The siege was only one incident among many in their lives and time had reduced it to a faint memory.

''An infinite number of infinitesimal changes'' marks the change from young girl to aging woman, and these Bennett traces without any effect of monotony. Both sisters grow steadily slower and less flexible in activities, emotions, sympathies, hopes, interests. Constance, realizing suddenly that Samuel, her husband, was nearly forty and that she had been married six years, reflects that nothing has happened. She had obtained a sure ascendency over her mother—not by seeking it, but just by the passing of time; she had acquired skill in the management of her household and her shop; she had constructed a chart of Samuel's individuality with the submerged rocks and perilous currents all carefully marked, so that she could voyage safely in those seas; and Fan, the puppy, whose entrance into a hitherto dogless home had been one of the revolutionary changes wrought by her marriage, was now a sedate and disillusioned dog, with a son in the house and grandchildren scattered over the town.

It is by giving us vividly the quality of certain moments of realization in the lives of the sisters that Bennett most effectively conveys the sense of the passing of the years. These are the moments when life seems to pause and to reveal something of its meaning to them, so that they think they understand what they have been living through and how they have changed since the last moment when they were fully conscious of themselves. Such a moment comes to Sophia, when as a young girl full of ambition and energy, she stands beside the bed of her paralytic father and listens to his prohibitions and his commands —this wreck, she suddenly realizes—dictating to her youth! And she is saddened into profound grief by the absurdity of the scene. In a momentary ecstasy of insight, she feels older than her father in her understanding of life. Pure pride of youth and joy of living possess Sophia driving with Gerald down the Champs Élyseés; with intense, throbbing emotion, she longs with painful ardor for more and more pleasure then and forever. Compare this simple ecstasy with the curiously complicated and subtle emotion, colored by reflection and disappointment, of the Sophia in the restaurant scene with Chirac. And then watch Sophia at fifty, looking out once again on the Square of her girlhood, remembering its aspect on winter mornings, remembering her own youth, finding it all beautiful and touching; and suddenly reflecting that not for millions of pounds would she live her life over again. Then the tragic moment, ten years later, when she is shocked into a kind of primitive emotion, uncolored by any moral or religious quality, by the sight of the dead old man who had been Gerald.

It made no difference that Gerald had wasted his life or caused her sorrow. What affected her was that he had once been young and that he had grown old and was now dead. Youth and vigor always came to that—everything came to that. "Yet a little while and I shall be lying on a bed like that. And what shall I have lived for? What is the meaning of it?" Constance, who in her more placid way had embraced more completely such experiences as came to her within the narrow limits of St. Luke's Square, ends not with the tragic question, but with a half-ironic affirmation. Old and alone and sick as she was—just a rheumatic old lady in the eyes of the rising generation—when she surveyed her life and life in general, she would think with a sort of tart but not sour cheerfulness, "Well, that is what life is."

Although Fossette is alone on the stage when the scene closes, there is no feeling of emptiness, for we have been kept aware of Constance's son and his friends, and Samuel Povey's nephew, and others of the generation that has been gradually coming to look on the two sisters as mere pathetic survivals from an earlier time. Life in the Five Towns moves on. And it moves on too in the old German town of Lübeck after the family of Buddenbrook, prominent in its merchant society for over a century, is exhausted and dying.

III

The movement of Thomas Mann's *Budden-brooks* is one of growth and decay through four generations. The curtain rises on a family gathering, about 1830—a hearty feast, with children, grandchildren, poor relations, old friends. "There they all sat, on heavy, high-backed chairs, consuming good heavy food from good heavy silver plate, drinking full-bodied wines and expressing their views freely on all subjects. When they began to talk shop, they slipped unconsciously more and more into dialect, and used the clumsy but comfortable idioms that seemed to embody to them the business efficiency and the easy well-being of their community." At the end, some fifty years later, there are a few aging, grief-stricken women, talking of the death of little Hanno, the delicate boy who should have carried on the family name. Hanno had been born when his father had brought the Buddenbrook fortunes to their highest point; when he was about to build an imposing new house and to be elected Senator. But the decline had already begun; the Senator felt himself losing his firm grip on events; and in a moment of sad clarity, he reminded his sister that "often the outward and visible material signs and symbols of happiness and success only show themselves when the process of decline has already set in; the outer mani-

festations take time—like the light of that star
up there, which may in reality be already
quenched, when it looks to us to be shining its
brightest.''

Little Hanno sees more of death than of birth
in the family, more losses than gains. When his
old governess says good-by to him, after his
father's death, ''his face wore the same brooding,
introspective look with which he had stood at his
father's death-bed, and his grandmother's bier,
witnessed the breaking-up of the great household,
and shared in so many events of the same kind,
though of lesser outward significance. The de-
parture of old Ida belonged to the same category
as other events with which he was already familiar; breakings-up, closings, endings, disinte-
grations—he had seen them all.'' And with a
characteristic little mannerism, he lifted his head
and seemed cautiously to sniff the air, as if he expected to catch ''that odour, that strange and yet
familiar odour which, at his grandmother's bier,
not all the scent of the flowers had been able to
disguise.'' In one of his short stories, Mann
speaks of an old merchant family that for generations had lived, worked and died in its fine old
gabled house; at the end it produced an artist or
two. And he adds, ''It often happens that a race
with dry, practical, bourgeois traditions, finds
itself again towards the end of its days in art.''
So it happens with the Buddenbrooks, for Hanno

is a gifted musician. So it seems to have happened with Mann's own family, for *Buddenbrooks* is—under the usual disguises of fiction—the story of his own family, patrician, conservative merchants of Lübeck.

As we read *Buddenbrooks*, his first novel, and the short stories collected in the *Death in Venice* volume, we become aware of Mann's deep concern with the problem of the artist—what he is, whether he is to be trusted or regarded with suspicion. His studies of artists are sometimes satirical, sometimes broadly humorous, sometimes deeply sympathetic, but always questioning. What is the truth of the artist's relation to himself and to society? As one reads these studies, one finds a certain pattern recurring significantly over and over again. The hero of *Death in Venice* is an author of distinguished fiction; on his father's side he comes of a family of officers and magistrates, men who lived severe, steady lives in the service of the state; but his mother was the daughter of a Bohemian music-master; "a marriage of sober, painstaking, conscientiousness, with the impulses of a darker, more fiery nature, had had an artist as its result." Tonio Kröger, artist hero of another story, is the son of a leading merchant in a North German city, and of a beautiful black-haired woman from the South, a musician. Tonio's story arises out of the conflict of impulses in his blood and the compelling need of reconciliation. Hanno Buddenbrook is a musician; his father had married a bride from Holland, with an exotic strain in her inheritance—a woman of musical, artistic gifts, quite different from the practical-minded German women around her.

The reason for Mann's preoccupation with this theme lies, as one would suspect, in his own heredity and his own deep-seated inner conflict. His father was such a German merchant of fine old traditions as he pictures in Thomas Buddenbrook; his mother a Portuguese lady. The two strains in his inheritance did not blend readily. The world of art, thought, music, is his world; but his artists are often troubled with a sense of their own feebleness in that world of practical, balanced, sane activity, of easy adjustment to the demands of society, where the German burghers moved so easily and with so much dignity. Mann can satirize the dullness, the materialism, the insensitiveness of the practical man; but he can also dissect the artist's posing, his self-preoccupation, his sickly introspection, his moral laxity and lack of dignity. Tonio Kröger confesses to sharing at times "all the suspicions against the typical artist which any of his respectable forefathers would have felt against a mountebank or strolling player who might have entered the house." He feels that the artist, who must stand apart from the human before he can play with it, present it coolly and impartially, is himself somewhat inhuman. "The gift for style, form, expression, already presupposes this cool and critical relationship with the human, even a certain human poverty and desolation." He finds literature more of a curse than a calling— a curse that begins to show itself early, at a time when one should by right still be living in peace and accord with God and the world. "You begin by feeling yourself set apart, in some mysterious antagonism to others, to the usual, the ordinary. The abyss of irony, disbelief, opposition, knowledge, feeling, which separates you from people, yawns deeper and deeper. . . . What a fate! Provided that your heart is sufficiently alive, sufficiently loving, to feel it as frightful." He concludes by confessing to a stealthy, devouring hankering after the bliss of mediocrity.

This love of the ordinary life, this yearning for the normal, the respectable, the likable, which Mann makes his Tonio express, is beautifully wrought into the structure of *Buddenbrooks*. It is a record of the common life, of ordinary people. Only Christian Buddenbrook, who might have been a comic actor, had there been any place for artists in the scheme of the family traditions, but who is only a marred business man and a hopeless hypochondriac; and little Hanno, who was too weak to bring his gift of music to fruition— only these two are markedly different from the other Buddenbrooks and the inhabitants of the north German town. The background of the family chronicle is the staid old Free City, with its granaries on the water front, its ships in the harbor, the gray-bearded craftsmen in the narrow shops built into the arcades of the market square, its fish-wives and dairy-women, its burgesses in the senate house, its grey Gothic buildings and gabled houses. On this background is woven the pattern of a closely-knit family life—births, celebrations, marriages, deaths, quarrels, scandals, ambitions, anniversaries. The family is the hero, the characters but cells in its organism.

Our perception of the continuous life of the family is sharpened by a device deftly employed by Mann: the family book of records, kept with religious care by the head of the family in each generation. Here is Consul Buddenbrook, early in the novel, recording the birth of his second daughter and piously thanking God for all his mercies. "The pen hurried glibly over the paper, with here and there a commercial flourish, talking with God in every line." Parenthetically he notes, "I have taken out an insurance policy for my youngest daughter, of one hundred and fifty thaler current. Lead her, O Lord, in Thy ways, give her a pure heart," and so on for several more pages. Sometimes the record has a deciding voice in the fate of some member of the family. Tony, the Consul's daughter, has fallen in love with a poor medical student whom her family will not permit her to marry. They do their best, in ways for the most part kindly, to cure her of this unfortunate fancy. They find for her a suitor of the prosperous merchant type of which they approve. But loathing the long golden whiskers of the importunate Herr Grünlich, she resists all their arguments and entreaties and thinks longingly of the student, so different from anyone she has ever known. Then one day in a mood of weary idleness, she turns over the pages of the family record, becomes absorbed in it, is impressed by the simple but stately chronicle style which mirrors the family attitude, its modest self-respect, its reverence for tradition. "No point in her own tiny past was lacking. Her birth, her childish illnesses, her first school, her confirmation—everything was carefully entered, with an almost reverent observation of facts, in the Consul's small, flowing, business hand. . . . What, she mused, would be entered in the future after her name? All that was yet to be written there would be conned by later members of the family, with a piety equal to her own. She leaned back sighing; her heart beat solemnly. . . . Like a link in a chain. . . . She was important precisely as a link in this chain. . . . Such was her significance—to share by deed and word in the history of her family." And Tony, looking long

70

at the blank space after the last entry under her name, at last picks up the pen, and with feverish decision, writes down the date of her betrothal to Herr Grünlich.

A generation later, little Hanno unconsciously draws the line of his own fate and that of his family. Finding the book open one day, amused by all the names and the odd flourishes of handwriting and the different colored inks, toying with his mother's gold pen, he finds his own name —Justus Johann Kaspar; and mechanically, dreamily, he draws a beautiful double line diagonally across the page, under his name. Questioned somewhat angrily by his father later as to what possessed him to do such a mischievous thing, Hanno stammers "I thought—I thought— there was nothing else coming."

Throughout the novel two characters hold our interest without a break, Tony and her brother Thomas, both children at the outset. Tony is charmingly drawn: a person of the type that does not develop but keeps her fundamental characteristics unchanged; she is spontaneous, resilient, emotional, naïve, intensely loyal to the family. Her little stock of general ideas she had acquired during her brief love-affair with the student, a young radical. And thereafter she had lovingly cherished them; and whenever she was thoughtful or felt that the occasion demanded some reflections upon life, she would produce these old ideas, with a touching faith in their truth and durability. At the death of her favourite brother Thomas, when his wife and son are unable to weep under the sudden shock, Tony surrenders herself utterly to one of the refreshing bursts of feeling which her happy nature always had at its command. "Her face still streamed with tears, but she was soothed and comforted and entirely herself as she rose to her feet and began straightway to occupy her mind with the announcements of the death—an enormous number of elegant cards, which must be ordered at once." Tony's two marriages are unlucky, her daughter's one attempt even more so: she is growing old with nothing left to console her in the decline of the family. But we leave her talking about life, making observations upon the past and the future—"though of the future there was in truth almost nothing to be said."

Strikingly different is her brother Thomas, a complicated character that steadily develops and subtly alters. In Thomas are impulses in conflict with the ordered, active, practical life of a merchant, which he, as head of the Buddenbrooks, is called upon to lead. He has some turn for introspection and some half-conscious yearnings for philosophy and art. But early in his life he is offended by the eccentricities of his brother Christian, the frustrated artist. He feels something indecent, undignified in Christian's endless concern with himself, endless self-analysis, and wearisome communicativeness. He tells Tony that he has thought a great deal about this curious and useless self-preoccupation, because he once had an inclination to it himself; but he observed that it made him unsteady, harebrained, incapable, and for him, control, equilibrium were the important things. In one of the quarrels between the brothers, Thomas cries, "I have become what I am because I did not want to become what you are. If I have inwardly shrunk from you, it has been because I needed to guard myself." He determines to be a good merchant, and he makes the impression on his fellow-townsmen of a successful man of action.

But the impulses that he starves out take their toll; the incessant hidden conflict going on below the surface fatally weakens him. Long before any signs are apparent to the outside observer, the process of disintegration is far advanced in him; and with this inner decay of Thomas himself, the decay of the great house keeps pace. His yearning for a kind of life different from that set before him by the family tradition leads him to make an unusual marriage with the daughter of a musician who is herself absorbed in music. His delicate only son is the very embodiment of all that was repressed in Thomas's nature. The relation between father and son is handled with subtlety and pathos: the disappointment of the

father who sees his hope that the son will suc-
ceed where he has failed gradually vanish, as the
boy turns away with distaste from all the studies
and activities that would develop him into a successful merchant. Hanno is happy only when he
slips into the music room to listen to his mother
and the church organist playing Bach fugues; or
when he sits up in the organ loft with Herr Pfühl,
high above the pastor in his pulpit, in the midst
of a mighty tempest of rolling sound. While the
sermon is going on, the two laugh softly at the
funny mannerisms of the pastor—for both were
of the opinion "that the sermon was silly twad-
dle, and that the real service consisted in that
which the Pastor and his congregation regarded
merely as a devotional accessory—the music."

Hoping to stimulate self-confidence in his son,
to make him realize the value and the interest of
intercourse with his fellows, the father sometimes took him on a round of visits, where he dis-
played his own tact and skill in dealing with each
person according to his character and position.
"But the little boy saw more than he should have
seen; the shy, gold-brown, blue-shadowy eyes observed too well. He saw not only the unerring
charm which his father exercised upon everybody; he saw as well, with strange and anguished
penetration, how cruelly hard it was upon him.
He saw how his father, paler and more silent
after each visit, would lean back in his corner of

the carriage with closed eyes and reddened eye-
lids; he realized with a sort of horror that on the
threshold of the next house a mask would glide
over his face, a galvanized activity take hold of
the weary frame. . . . And when he thought that
some day he should be expected to perform the
same part, under the gaze of the whole community, Hanno shut his eyes and shivered with re-
bellion and disgust." Once in a while when the
father involuntarily betrays some movement of
fear or suffering, Hanno meets his gaze with a
comprehension beyond his years: "Hanno might
fail his father in all that demanded vitality, energy, and strength. But where fear and suffering were in question, there Thomas Buddenbrook
could count on the devotion of his son."

The hopeful, hearty confidence in life and
growth that breathes through the earlier fortunes
of the Buddenbrooks has been lost in this exquisite but morbid sensibility.

Something of the effect of drama is secured by
the steady ascent, the climax, and the decline of
this family, as if it were in a struggle with time,
like the tragic hero's struggle with destiny. Yet
the dominant impression at the end is of the
"cycle of birth and growth, death and birth
again"—of time flowing on past the beholder,
"over all the barriers that might have marked
its end."

CHAPTER III
THE WILD GOOSE: VIRGINIA WOOLF'S
PURSUIT OF LIFE

Few novelists have exercised their critical intelligence on the art of fiction to the same degree as Virginia Woolf. *Mr. Bennett and Mrs. Brown,* a provocative address delivered at Cambridge University in 1924, and "Phases of Fiction," three articles published in *The Bookman* in 1929, not to mention many book reviews, make it possible to examine her own fiction in the light of her opinions about fiction. But if we expect to find convenient critical formulas, we are disappointed. Writing an acute review of the stories of Ernest Hemingway, and moving forward to conclusions with assurance, she yet disconcerts us somewhat at the end by making a reservation, both candid and ironic: "So we sum him up. So we reveal some of the prejudices, the instincts, and the fallacies out of which what it pleases us to call criticism is made." In *Phases of Fiction* she professes to be doing nothing more than to show a mind—her own—at work upon a shelfful of novels, and to let us watch it as it chooses and rejects, making itself a dwelling-place in accordance with its own appetite. On the mind of every reader of fiction, some design has been traced which reading brings to light. "Desires, ap-

VIRGINIA WOOLF

petites, however we may come by them, fill it in,
scoring now in this direction, now in that.'' The
world we create in this way is always in process
of creation and it is, she admits, a personal world,
possibly not habitable by other people; created in
obedience to tastes which may be peculiar to one
temperament and distasteful to another. Now it
may as well be said at the outset that unless some
designs have been traced upon our minds by what
is loosely called culture, Virginia Woolf's fiction
will touch them in vain. Her own mind is a finely
educated one; and she has been accused, by
people who, as Clive Bell* says, ''are not particularly well off for either culture or intellect,'' of
possessing a ''cultivated and intellectual'' style.
An intelligent person whose mind is not particularly cultivated may come to enjoy a cultivated
and intellectual style like that of Henry James.
He is deliberate, he provides all the necessary
transitions, his references are explicit enough to
make us at least aware that he is referring to
something a cultivated mind ought to know, and
it is always possible to hold fast to the thread of
a carefully plotted story. His novels, however
elaborate the psychology, are in the traditional
form. But the movements of Mrs. Woolf's mind
are swift and unpredictable. One must leap with
it from one point to the next, without seeking a

* Article on Virginia Woolf in *The Dial.*

bridge. She herself says of T. S. Eliot's poetry that its obscurity comes from intolerance of the old usages and politenesses of society—"respect for the weak, consideration for the dull." After flying precariously like an acrobat from bar to bar, she begins to envy the indolence of her ancestors, who instead of spinning madly through mid-air, dreamed quietly in the shade with a book. Her feeling about T. S. Eliot is precisely that of many readers about her.

Fundamentally dull people will not like Virginia Woolf, says Clive Bell, who admits that he likes her very much. Nor will people whose minds are neat and orderly and practical. Nor very emotional people who seek in fiction chiefly emotional release through identification. But many others, who find an initial difficulty, can overcome it simply by paying a little attention to their own undirected reveries—by exploring the stream of their own consciousness. "Miscellaneous, vague, chaotic, composed of memories, moods, sensations, and desires mingled helter-skelter with things tragic and comic, trivial and important treading upon the heels of one another, the stream goes continuously on from the moment we wake until it trails off fainter and fainter into slumber or death." * The need to make practical decisions of all sorts halts our

* J. W. Krutch, review of "Mrs. Dalloway," *The Nation*, June 3, 1925.

daydreaming and controls our thinking for periods long or short; the need of justifying our actions and opinions to ourselves and others compels the process called rationalizing; and once in a blue moon our thinking may become impersonal and creative. Outside the circle of awareness altogether lie those regions explored by a Dostoevsky or a D. H. Lawrence, where lurk the origins of moods and desires, the strange world outside the focus of consciousness. This world Mrs. Woolf seldom enters. It is our reveries, which psychologists have called the fundamental index of character, that fascinate her and that she chooses to record.

About 1917, Mrs. Woolf, who had been writing critical reviews for *The London Times Literary Supplement,* but had also been experimenting with imaginative sketches and stories, published in the Hogarth Press *The Mark on the Wall*—a daydream, a bit of the stream of consciousness. The daydreamer looks at a mark on the wall. Too indolent to get up and examine it, she allows her mind to drift without a rudder, to follow up any association; only now and then when it drifts into a dull backwater, she brings it back to the mark and starts afresh. Let anyone who has not played the eavesdropper upon his own consciousness in these off moments try this device of intermittently focussed reverie. He will probably not find floating on his own stream objects as de-

lightful and fantastic as Mrs. Woolf fishes up
from hers. But he will begin to comprehend the
value of reverie as an instrument of character
portrayal; he will find things out about himself,
amusing, disconcerting, and very instructive.
. . . Even if she examined that mark, thinks the
daydreamer, she might not be sure what it was
. . . living is such an accidental affair . . . just
think of the things we lose in a lifetime—and a
dozen incongruous objects, bird cages, jewels, coal
scuttles, that have disappeared at different times,
recur to memory; and make her wonder that she
has any clothes on her back. And that calls up a
comparison of living to being blown through the
tube at fifty miles an hour and landing at the
other end without even a hairpin left—"shot out
at the feet of God entirely naked—tumbling head
over heels in the asphodel meadows like brown
paper parcels pitched down a shoot in the post-
office" . . . and then after life . . . a poetic
image or two drifting off into vagueness, and then
she looks again at the mark. Perhaps it is a bit
of dust—"the dust which, so they say, buried
Troy three times over, only fragments of pots
refusing annihilation." Then feeling herself
sinking into drowsiness, she catches at the first
idea that passes—Shakespeare, sitting in an
armchair looking at the fire—and she sketches a
scene in a historical novel, which presently bores
her. (But it is interesting that just this scene

reappears after ten years as a part of Mrs. Woolf's *Orlando*.) And looking again at the mark, she thinks it projects from the wall and may be a tiny mound—a smooth tumulus like those barrows on the South Downs that are either tombs or camps . . . and she wonders about antiquaries who investigate such matters. What sort of man is an antiquary? "Retired Colonels for the most part, I daresay, leading parties of aged labourers to the top here, examining clods of earth and stone, and getting into correspondence with the neighboring clergy, which, being opened at breakfast time, gives them a feeling of importance, and the comparison of arrowheads necessitates cross-country journeys to the county towns, an agreeable necessity both to them and to their elderly wives, who wish to make plum jam or to clean out the study, and have every reason for keeping that great question of the camp or the tomb in perpetual suspension, while the Colonel himself feels agreeably philosophic in accumulating evidence on both sides of the question. It is true that he does finally incline to believe in the camp; and, being opposed, indites a pamphlet which he is about to read at the quarterly meeting of the local society when a stroke lays him low, and his last conscious thoughts are not of wife or child, but of the camp and that arrowhead there, which is now in the case at the local museum, together with the foot of a Chinese murderess, a handful of Elizabethan nails, a great many Tudor clay pipes, a piece of Roman pottery, and the wine-glass that Nelson drank out of—proving I really don't know what . . ." *

Proving at least the fertility of Mrs. Woolf's own mind in whimsical speculation, and preparing us for the sort of thing that happens in her novels, though it happens there under control and for a purpose. In *Jacob's Room*, for instance, Jacob is absorbed in certain studies he is carrying on at the British Museum, and we must be steeped in that atmosphere. So we see not only Jacob, but the odd people who sit near him, and we feel the queer minds clicking away near his: Miss Marchmont in her old plush dress and her claret-colored wig, with her gems and her chilblains and her philosophy, which she sometimes puts into pamphlets and gives away . . . and thinking of how Queen Alexandra once acknowledged a pamphlet of hers, she shifts in her seat and knocks over some books into Jacob's lap— which he was too absorbed to notice. "But Fraser, the atheist, on the other side, detesting plush, more than once accosted with leaflets, shifted irritably. He abhorred vagueness—the Christian religion, for example, and old Dean Parker's pronouncements. Dean Parker wrote books and Fraser utterly destroyed them by force of logic and left his children unbaptized—his

* *Monday and Tuesday.* The Hogarth Press. 1921.

wife did it secretly in the washing-basin—but Frazer ignored her, and went on supporting blasphemers, distributing leaflets, getting up his facts in the British Museum, always in the same check suit and fiery tie, but pale, spotted, irritable. Indeed, what a work—to destroy religion!'' And meanwhile Jacob transcribed a passage from Marlowe. We have never met Frazer before, we never meet him again. He impinged upon Jacob's life for a few minutes, and Mrs. Woolf pursued him for a paragraph, and achieved her usual effect —of making us feel excited about life, with all its queer juxtapositions and contrasts and incongruities.

II

This paragraph about Frazer suggests what Mrs. Woolf means when she talks about the novelist's interest in people. All of us have to be interested in people and in character for practical purposes, but novelists continue to be interested long after all practical needs have been served. ''The study of character becomes to them an absorbing pursuit; to impart character an obsession.'' A little old lady sits in the corner of a railway carriage—some Mrs. Brown—saying in effect, ''Come and catch me if you can.'' The novelist pursues this will-of-the-wisp, and perhaps in the end has to be content with a scrap of

VIRGINIA WOOLF

her dress or a strand of her hair. But success in the pursuit is the test of a novelist's achievement. The one way not to catch Mrs. Brown is the way, according to Mrs. Woolf, that became enormously popular with novelists of the early twentieth century—excellent novelists, too, in their way,—the Wellses, Bennetts, Galsworthys. They laid heavy stress upon details of environment to explain character: on the wages people received, what they could buy with them and where, what sorts of houses they lived in and whether they owned them or paid rent, and what amusements were open to them, what diseases they died of or recovered from, what servants they had and how they treated them. If Mr. Bennett saw Mrs. Brown in the railway carriage, he would note every detail: "He would notice the advertisements . . . the way in which the cushions bulged between the buttons; how Mrs. Brown wore a brooch which had cost three-and-ten-three at Whitworth's bazaar; and had mended both gloves—indeed the thumb of the left-hand glove had been replaced. And he would observe at length how this was the non-stop train from Windsor which calls at Richmond for the convenience of middle-class residents, who can afford to go to the theatre, but have not reached the social rank which can afford motor-cars, though it is true there are occasions (he would tell us what), when they hire them from a company (he would tell us

which).''* And the public has been so thoroughly
trained to expect that this is the way to learn
about characters in novels, that unless you tell
them firmly all about the houses and parents and
servants and hot water-bottles and gloves of old
women, they won't know that they are old women.
But that particular tool for fashioning character
is unsatisfactory to Mrs. Woolf, and she thinks
it beginning to be unsatisfactory to many readers.
With all this insistence on the fabric of things,
there is Mrs. Brown, still in her corner, not imagi-
natively realized at all, though we know all the
facts about her. A way of telling the truth about
people must be found—a new way, because there
are new truths we have become aware of.† Mrs.
Woolf is gaily dogmatic and a little unfair to her
elders in these comments, but she is right in insisting that those younger novelists who are not
merely following well-worn traditions have been
trying to express their sense of life and character
in new terms. From some of their experiments,
she admits, Mrs. Brown emerges disheveled and
pale. But somehow or other she must be rescued
and set before us.

* *Mr. Bennett and Mrs. Brown.*

† In discussing Dostoevsky, May Sinclair, and D. H. Lawrence,
in *Dead Reckonings in Fiction,* we saw how hard it was to convey some of these new truths, without making us feel as if we
were watching the dissection of laboratory specimens.

VIRGINIA WOOLF

III

So we have seen Mrs. Woolf as critic insisting upon success in characterization as the prime essential of the novelist's art. We have seen that she is dissatisfied with certain well-worn tools of the craft and disposed to experiment, and we have noted her peculiar aptitude in handling reverie. No wonder the reverie process fascinates her—it would anyone whose mind worked like hers. What she says of Laurence Sterne is often true of herself: "It is his own mind that fascinates him, its oddities and its whims, its fancies and its sensibilities; and it is his own mind that colors the book and gives it walls and shape." Of her novels, *Mrs. Dalloway* has seemed to critics the outcome of deliberate experiment with a new method. In her preface to the Modern Library edition, she denies that. It was true, she says, that she was dissatisfied with the form of fiction in vogue; or rather, dissatisfied with nature for "giving an idea, without providing a house for it to live in." The novel was the obvious lodging, but was, it seemed, built on the wrong plan. So her idea "started as the oyster starts or the snail to secrete a house for itself. And this it did without any conscious direction. The little note-book in which an attempt was made to forecast a plan was soon abandoned, and the book grew day by day, week by week, without any plan at all, except that which was dictated each morning in the act of writing.'' Let us regard Mrs. Dalloway of the novel as the Mrs. Brown of the moment, whom Mrs. Woolf is trying to capture, and see how she is put into a book.

Clarissa Dalloway is one of the nice people she writes about. For her characters are almost as civilized and as free from eccentricities and obsessions as those of Jane Austen; almost as correct in their behavior as those of Henry James. Mrs. Dalloway is fifty, moves in good society, likes to entertain, is gracious, and something of a snob. We share with her one day, which ends with a party, and catch glimpses of that same day in the lives of people casually or intimately connected with her. She goes out in the morning —in the West End of London—to buy flowers for her party; waits for a royal carriage to pass. Septimus Smith, a shell-shocked soldier, is standing near her. She returns, talks with her maid; an old lover, Peter Walsh, unexpectedly calls. He is just back from India to make arrangements to marry a young grass widow he thinks he loves. Richard, her husband, comes in after a lunch with Lady Bruton, bringing her flowers; her daughter Elizabeth goes out with her grim history tutor, whom Mrs. Dalloway dislikes intensely because of her curious fascination for Elizabeth. All of these little events stir thoughts, memories, associations, that light up her character, her present, her past. She successfully carries off her party, and at midnight it is over. Peter is almost as fully portrayed. After seeing Clarissa, he walks in Regent Park, his mind and emotions stirred to unusual activity. He looks up at an airplane, tracing an advertisement of toffee across the sky; and Septimus, the soldier, also looks up, and later sits near him in the park, with his young Italian wife. A few hours afterward Peter passes by the house where an ambulance has just stopped to pick up the body of Septimus, who has thrown himself out of the window to escape the psychiatrist who is planning to send him to a sanatorium. Peter has dinner at his hotel, goes to the party, sees Sally Seton, who used to visit Clarissa years ago, when Peter was in love with her. At last he has a chance to speak with Clarissa, and he knows that he still loves her and will never marry the young woman in India. Septimus's fate has been decided in that twelve hours, and Peter's too. The psychiatrist who frightened Septimus into suicide comes to Clarissa's party, and mentions the sad case. Clarissa feels a chill —death at her party. In an earlier version, Mrs. Woolf tells us, Septimus didn't exist; it was Clarissa who was to kill herself, or merely die at the end of the party. But somehow Septimus grew into the pattern, and in some strange way is Clarissa's double. He has slipped beneath the surface where she still keeps her footing. "She felt somehow very like him—the young man who had killed himself. She felt glad he had done it —thrown it away." She sees how the meaning of her own life has been defaced by corruption, lies, chatter; how she had schemed, valued success. Septimus in his recklessness has preserved something she has lost. His death was a defiance of the obscure evil represented by men like Sir William Bradshaw, the psychiatrist—men who exert an intolerable force upon the soul. Somehow it was her disaster that the young man had killed himself, and she forced to stand there in evening dress, receiving guests. But going to the window, she draws back the curtains and watches the old lady in the house across the way preparing for bed. With all the noise and chatter of the drawing-room behind her, it was fascinating to have this glimpse of a life quietly going its way. Somehow the shock of death has made Clarissa feel the beauty and strangeness and excitement of life more intensely, and she turns back to her party with a certain zest.

The book is a composition of reverie and dialogue, with brief snapshots of the outer aspect of people and things. We have the stream of consciousness and the stream of events. There are long reveries of Clarissa and of Peter, shifting as they notice things about them, or as a chance stimulus brings up a memory, or as they maké some contact with people. When the char-

acters are in groups, there is a symphony of reverie and dialogue—what they say aloud, and
what is drifting through their minds at the same
moment. And sometimes Mrs. Woolf draws completely away from her characters, as in the passage inspired by the grey nurse who sits knitting
beside the dozing Peter in Regent Park. While
Peter sleeps, why shouldn't his creator play with
her own mind?

What is the result? Has the character of Mrs.
Dalloway been successfully projected? At the
end Peter feels a curious stir at the sight of
Clarissa coming towards him: "What is it that
fills me with extraordinary excitement? It is
Clarissa, he said. For there she was." Clarissa
is emphatically. But there is nothing about which
readers differ more than the so-called reality of
characters; and perhaps for some readers she
isn't. She may come to life for some of us, because we want her to. She satisfies a desire.
Here is a woman over fifty for whom life is still
exciting. She isn't dying of cancer or threatened
with a stroke or suffering strange distortions of
character from repressions; she is not an object
of contempt or ridicule; her husband still loves
her, her old lover still feels the attraction of her
personality; she isn't consciously or unconsciously
sacrificing her daughter, nor is she being sacri-
ficed by her. In short she offers an extension of
experience that makes the prospect of fifty years

old less desolating than it is usually made to appear in fiction; and we may want to have the illusion of a pleasant life at fifty just as much as at other times we may want to relive it at twenty. Then Clarissa is a person we like to believe in because Mrs. Woolf endows her with her own sense of life, as a fascinating pattern of the significant and irrelevant, odd, confused, incoherent, with sudden flashes of meaning. Clarissa always had the feeling that "it was very dangerous to live, even one day." In one of her moments of self-justification she thinks, "Peter believes me to be a snob, for liking people around me, and Richard regards it as foolish to like excitement when it is bad for my heart . . . but both are wrong." "What she liked was simply life. 'That's what I do it for,' she said, speaking aloud to life." And Clarissa has the revelatory glimpses: "Then for that moment she had seen an illumination; a match burning in a crocus; an inner meaning almost expressed."

IV

The impression Mrs. Woolf gives of the trivial, tragic, confused, lovely, queer mix-up we call life is in one way disappointing, because it leaves us more at a loss than ever for a principle of order. And one of the satisfactions of art is that it simplifies confusion by selecting only certain forms and colors for its design. If by wearing blinkers and seeing only a few aspects of things, we have been able to persuade ourselves that we perceive an order and a meaning, Mrs. Woolf comes along and makes us face the infinite complications of the material. She exposes her reader to "constellations of stimuli," which form patterns of many motifs, the shape and color of each depending largely upon its relationship to each part of the whole design. The result—sometimes, at any rate,—is that we become excited at the thought of living in so bewildering a world; and this too is pleasurable, though not soothing like the illusion of simplicity and order. Every now and then, we are enough shaken out of our habitual routine to catch a glimpse of life as Mrs. Woolf characteristically sees it. Here is a day, for instance, on which a young newspaper reporter, a girl, was faced with the problem of what to do with a desperately sick friend. The problem was complicated by lack of money, by an estrangement between the friend and her family, and by the obligation of the reporter to carry out, no matter what happened, certain assignments for her paper. Part of the day was taken up with telephone calls, long waits for the doctor—who, as it was Sunday and he was getting old, didn't want to come unless he could be sure it was a real crisis; killing time between preparing ice-packs and broths and taking temperatures, by reading the Yiddish comic strip of the newspaper. Then the sudden irruption of ambulance men, who were rough and hurried because it was late and they hadn't had their supper; the impotent rage of the reporter at the irrelevant intrusion of the ambulance men's supper into her tragic situation; attempts of a friend to reason with her—"But even ambulance men must eat!" Then waiting at the hospital, with a vista of two long wards during visiting hour, certain groups, gestures, sounds, stamping themselves on the mind: a woman incessantly trying to lift her hands, and three men, one a policeman, mechanically pushing them down. A talkative woman, also waiting, explains everything: "Her husband the policeman wants to be alone with her, but her brothers say, 'Ain't we a right to be here too?'" Shrieks of laughter from convalescent patients; a homely girl in a hideous grey dressing gown, walking about, grinning, and sucking a thermometer. A sense of the comedies and tragedies of a score of lives, suddenly broken off and lost forever by the need to dash to Brooklyn and "cover" a church meeting. Subway confusion, suburban streets dimly lighted, a half-empty church, decorous people, seeming lifeless after the movement and suffering of the hospital, a plump minister droning out a moth-eaten psychology of prayer, a correct usher in frock coat pointing out the hymn to the harassed young reporter—something about throwing all your cares on Jesus—her expression of dangerous irritation,

for if it was exasperating that ambulance men
have to eat suppers, it is unbearable that people
should sing hymns in the outskirts of Brooklyn.
Another dash through subways to the newspaper
office to write up copy. Ten-thirty at night. Elevator man asleep in the elevator, the cat playing
with scraps of paper. Upstairs a glaringly lighted
littered room, a few tired reporters in shirt
sleeves, feet on tables, the spasmodic weary
clicking of two or three typewriters. All these
universes—the hospital, the church, the newspaper office; all these lives brushing against one
another, glimpsed for an instant; all the movement and the incoherent scraps of conversation.
And one's own stream of consciousness flowing
steadily on. Only such a method as Mrs. Woolf's
can render the intimate "feel" of such a day's
experience. And it must create the impression of
irrelevance and incoherence without being either
irrelevant or incoherent.

v

This method is perfectly exemplified in *Mrs.
Dalloway*, which seems to be the successful outcome of experiments carried on in *The Mark on
the Wall, The Voyage Out,* and *Jacob's Room.
(Night and Day,* Mrs. Woolf's second novel, is
entirely traditional in form.) Yet if one is seeking interesting people to read about, Rachel and
some of the other characters in *The Voyage*

97

Out, and Jacob in *Jacob's Room,* might be preferred to Mrs. Dalloway, who, with all her insight
and grace, is rather limited—lacking in force and
originality, deficient in passion, accepting too
easily the standards of her own set. Whereas
Jacob and Rachel, both of whom die young, seem
full of latent possibilities. The theme of *The
Voyage Out* is the awakening of Rachel, who is
undeveloped and immature at twenty-four, feeling nothing deeply except her music. She is quite
willing to accept the people around her as symbols merely, of age, of motherhood, of learning;
she cares little about getting into communication
with them. "To feel anything strongly was to
create an abyss between oneself and others, who
feel strongly perhaps, but differently. . . . It
was far better to play the piano and forget and
rest." She takes a voyage on a cargo ship with
her father, a ship owner, and a few other passen-
gers—her aunt, her uncle, a Greek scholar, and
the Dalloways (who bear little resemblance to
their namesakes in the later novel). Mr. Dalloway, yielding to a casual impulse, kisses Rachel.
That experience, and the subsequent discussion
of it with her aunt, mark the beginning of her
coming alive. People, she realizes, could cease to
be symbols, could become exciting. And presently
her aunt, who had not found much to attract her
in Rachel, notices a change and begins to draw her
out, in her humorous detached way, and to suggest

VIRGINIA WOOLF

to her that she might become a person on her own account. "The vision of her own personality, of herself as a real everlasting thing, different from anything else, unmergeable, like the sea or the wind, flashed into Rachel's mind, and she became profoundly excited at the thought of living." (The Dalloways, by the way, debark at the next port, and figure no more in the story.) Rachel stays for many weeks with her aunt at a sea-coast resort somewhere in South America, while her father pursues his business in the interior. Near the villa is a hotel, with a miscellaneous crowd of shifting guests, mostly English, there on business or for a holiday. Rachel is drawn into a dance at the hotel, then into a picnic on the mountain. She unfolds more and more. Young Hewet falls in love with her. They go with a party on a week's excursion up the river into the jungle, and the relationship with Hewet develops. Then with the incoherence of life, Rachel contracts typhoid fever and dies. The voyage out takes on tragic significance: a literal voyage out to South America, then the voyaging out of Rachel's adventuring personality, finally a voyage out of life altogether.

Then there is Jacob Flanders: a little boy playing on the beach, a young boy collecting butterflies and beetles, a youth going to Cambridge in October, 1906; taking a cruise to the Scilly Isles on his vacation, spending a week-end at a country

99

VIRGINIA WOOLF

house with his college friends, living in rooms in
London, going to a Bohemian party, having a
casual love affair with the brainless pretty little
Florinda who deceives him, studying in the
British Museum, making fashionable calls, riding
on busses in Holborn, going to Greece and falling
in love with Greek art—and also with an experienced married lady—doing in short what almost any young Englishman of good social position and not much money, and a little more than
average intelligence but no extraordinary gifts,
might do. Then the War and a swift end. Is
Mrs. Woolf really trying to protray the character
of Jacob? Perhaps the title is meant to suggest
something different,—not Jacob, but his room;
the place where he lives, all his surroundings, ani-
mate and inanimate, upon which he acts and
which act on him; all the atmospheres he
breathed. An elderly lady sits opposite him in
the train, and he lifts her dressing-case down from
the rack for her; she wonders who he is, but
never knows. While he stands at his window, he
sees a little girl stand on tiptoe to post a letter
in the pillar-box. When he is riding on the top
of a bus, he watches an errand boy swing down
the bus steps and dodging between the cars, dis-
appear forever in the crowd. We see him hurry-
ing across a court at Cambridge, late at night,
the only person passing at that moment; his foot-
steps echoing back from Chapel, from Hall, from
100

Library—"The old stone echoing, 'the young
man, the young man, back to his rooms.'" We
see his room at Cambridge when he is absent,
though his personality prevades it: "Listless is
the air in an empty room; just swelling the curtain; the flowers in the jar shift. One fibre in the
wicker arm-chair creaks, though no one sits
there." Several things happen at the same
moment about sunset on a spring day just before
the War. They are flashed swiftly before us:
Jacob rises from a chair in Hyde Park where he
has been idling, and tearing up his ticket, walks
away; the windows of Kensington Palace flushed
fiery rose; "Jacob," wrote Mrs. Flanders, with
the red light on her page, "is hard at work after
his delightful journey"; "The Kaiser," the far-
away voice remarked in Whitehall, "received me
in audience." And that last, of course, suggests
the coming War and the end of Jacob. But before he passes out of sight, his old tutor catches
a glimpse of him walking down Piccadilly, remembers the set of Byron he gave the lad, thinks
what a fine young man he has become; and Clara
Durant, who loves him and knows he does not
love her, starts at a glimpse of him in the crowd
going in to a concert. When his mother and his
friend are going through his possessions after
his death, and his mother stands helplessly wondering what to do with an old pair of shoes, the
sentence quoted above recurs: "Listless is the air

in an empty room. . . .'' Now Jacob's room is really empty.

Less unified in effect than *Mrs. Dalloway, Jacob's Room* is like a succession of reveries, focussed on Jacob. It is as if someone said— Jacob Flanders? Oh yes, that young man who was killed at the beginning of the War. I remember when he was a little boy and picked up that old sheep's skull on the beach . . . and so on, one association calling up another—people, places, pictures, rumors—discursive, loosely chronological, speculative about the meaning of it all. Isn't Virginia Woolf using Jacob—as in a miniature way she used the mark on the wall— to convey her sense of the queerness and the fascination of life? ''The strange thing about life is that though the nature of it must have been apparent to everyone for hundreds of years, no one has left any adequate account of it.'' * One begins to suspect that the Mrs. Brown she is pursuing is not any Jacob or Rachel or Mrs. Dalloway, but life itself. If it were Jacob himself that she were mainly concerned with—as for instance with Conrad or Dostoevsky it is Nostromo or Ivan Karamazov—we should feel an overwhelming sense of the tragic futility of his end. One doesn't hear of readers weeping over Jacob.

* *Jacob's Room.*

What about *To the Lighthouse,* the novel which
followed *Mrs. Dalloway?* One personality does
emerge—Mrs. Ramsay, the organizing and pre-
siding spirit of the house in the Hebrides that her
family of husband and eight children and their
numerous guests filled to overflowing in the
summers before the War. In the first part, *The
Window,* Mrs. Ramsay is seated at a window
amusing her youngest boy James with stories,
while Lily Briscoe, an artist guest, is outside
painting the scene, and Mr. Ramsay stalks up
and down past the window, reciting scraps of
poetry when he reaches rough places in his philosophic speculations, and other guests and
members of the family drift past on their own
business. Through glimpses of Mrs. Ramsay's
stream of consciousness we build up the picture
of her character, her life, her feeling about everyone connected with her. We also share Lily's
reveries and dip briefly into those of other characters. The method is that of *Mrs. Dalloway,*
but even more expert and more beautiful in style.
James hopes they will be able to sail to the lighthouse tomorrow; his whole being is concentrated
on that desire; he hates his father for announcing
that the weather will be bad, and for distracting
his mother's attention from himself. "He hated
him for interrupting them; he hated him for the

exaltation and sublimity of his gestures; for the
magnificence of his head; for his exactness and
egotism (for there he stood, commanding them to
attend to him); but most of all he hated the
twang and twitter of his father's emotion, which,
vibrating around them, disturbed the perfect
simplicity and good sense of his relations with
his mother.'' Not that James understood all that
—he simply felt it would be a pleasure to kill his
father with the scissors he was cutting out pictures with. They all dine that evening in the
candle-lighted room, Mrs. Ramsay bringing the
whole group of separate and constrained individ-
ualities together by her tact; ''the whole effort of
merging and flowing and creating rested on her.''
In the evening she has a quiet hour or two with
her husband, who relies upon her absolutely for
the sympathy his ego demands. All of these people
to some degree lean on Mrs. Ramsay, and that
gives her at times a pleasant sense of power.
She has the social charm of Mrs. Dalloway, with
a deeper and richer nature.

They don't go to the lighthouse. Years pass,
and the house remains empty except for the oc-
casional visits of the old caretaker. Nothing
happens as Mrs. Ramsay had thought it would.
The engagement of two young guests—which she
had engineered a bit—ends in an unhappy
marriage. Her favourite daughter Prue dies in
childbirth; her gifted son Andrew is destroyed in

a moment by a shell in the War; Mrs. Ramsay herself dies rather suddenly one night. Ten years later some of the same guests, those of the children who are left, and Mr. Ramsay, gather again in the house, rescued from decay by the heroic efforts of the old cleaning women; and James at last goes to the lighthouse—against his will, hating his father for making them go just as he had hated him before for standing in the way. But against his will, too, he is pleased when his father praises him for his skill in steering the boat. In the effort James makes in the boat to fix a fugitive impression connected somehow with the lighthouse and with the actual and vaguely remembered hatred of his father—this effort to fish something up from the deeps of memory—we see how his father's attitude that evening years before towards the trip and towards his mother had fixed James's relation to his father.

The handling of reverie is even more deft than in *Mrs. Dalloway*. Take the pages where Mrs. Ramsay is reading from Grimm the story of the fisherman and his wife, allowing her thoughts to drift, now and again taking a turn suggested by the story: "The story of the Fisherman and his Wife was like the bass gently accompanying a tune, which now and then ran up unexpectedly into the melody." There is a typical example of how fantastically several strands of thought are twisted together in reverie, when Mrs. Ramsay is walking in the garden with her husband, thinking about him and his work and his problems, and about her own duties as housekeeper and gardener: "She must stop for a moment to see whether those were fresh mole-hills on the bank; then, she thought, stooping down to look, a great mind like his must be different in every way from ours. All the great men she had ever known, she thought, deciding that a rabbit must have got in, were like that, and it was good for young men (though the atmosphere of lecture-rooms was stuffy and depressing to her beyond endurance almost) simply to hear him, simply to look at him. But without shooting rabbits, how was one to keep them down? . . ."

In estimating Mrs. Woolf's accomplishment in characterizing people by this special technique of hers, it is important to notice with what skill she conveys marked differences in temperament. The reveries of her characters are as distinct and individual as the gestures, mannerisms of speech, tones of voice, that other novelists rely upon for identification. James Joyce, Marcel Proust, Dorothy Richardson, all experts in the recording of reveries, make us feel that we are constantly in personal and intimate contact with the consciousness of the author; so that the use of this method has seemed to imply a highly subjective type of writing. But open *To the Lighthouse* upon any passage of reverie, and there will be no mistaking Tansley's for Lily's, or Mrs. Ramsay's for her husband's, or James's for his sister Cam's. We see their minds as objectively as with a Dickens we might see their facial expression or the movement of their hands. Lily the artist, for instance, thinks in sharp visual images; the abstract must receive a concrete embodiment before she can deal with it. Told by Mrs. Ramsay's son that his father was always speculating about subject, object, and the nature of reality, she asked what he meant precisely, and he said, "Oh, think of a kitchen table when you're not there." So Lily usually sees a scrubbed deal table when the thought of Mr. Ramsay's books drifts into her mind, and this phantom table has a way of lodging itself in the fork of a pear tree, its four legs in air, if she happens to be in the orchard; or in some other ridiculous place. All of us are intermittently engaged in self-justification, but we all have our individual ways of accomplishing this universal need; and Mrs. Woolf gives to the reveries of all her characters both this universal and this individual stamp. She has created only one character who seems to be the vehicle of her own reveries—Orlando, who lives through three centuries and two sexes and many adventures and pursuits, and whose consciousness is ample enough to contain Mrs. Woolf's.

If one wonders whether the aim of these novels is really to create character, the wonder is not

VIRGINIA WOOLF

lessened by *To the Lighthouse,* in spite of the
vividness of Mrs. Ramsay. The first movement
of the book brings out the interrelationships of
the various people in the old house and stresses
the integrating quality of Mrs. Ramsay's personality, which draws the whole group together.
But then follows the next movement, *Time Passes.*
There is only an empty house, visited by the
winds and storms of many winters, stroked at
regular intervals by the beams from the lighthouse, falling into decay from damp and dust,
until it is touch and go with it whether the process of decay will be completed and the house will
pitch down into darkness. A pair of shoes, a
shooting cap, some faded skirts in wardrobes—
things people had shed and left—these alone kept
the human shape. Memories of Mrs. Ramsay
lingering about the house come to life only when
the old cleaning women recall this or that trivial
detail about her, and then "faint and flickering,
like a yellow beam or the circle at the end of a
telescope, a lady in a grey cloak, stooping over
her flowers, went wandering over the bedroom
wall, up the dressing-table, across the washstand,
as Mrs. McNab hobbled and ambled, dusting and
straightening." The procession of nights and
days and seasons passes before us in imagery so
beautiful that it would be hard to find in twentieth
century English prose anything to surpass it.
And what happens to the human beings who had

peopled the house is lightly touched on in a paren-
thesis here and there, like a poetic or ironic mark
of punctuation in the long record of time. For
example, there are nights full of wind and destruction when the sea tosses and the restless
sleeper wakes and is tempted to ask questions as
to the what and why and wherefore of things.
"[Mr. Ramsay, stumbling along a passage one
dark night, stretched his arms out, but Mrs.
Ramsay, having died rather suddenly the night
before, his arms, though stretched out, remained
empty.]" Lovely summer days drift by; sunsets
on the sea, fishing boats against the moon, se-
renity. Then the apparition of an ashen-colored
ship, come, gone; a purplish stain upon the bland
surface of the sea, as if something had boiled
and bled invisibly beneath. "[Mr. Carmichael
brought out a volume of poems that spring which
had an unexpected success. The war, people
said, had revived their interest in poetry.]"

And so one day the house, rescued, is reopened.
It is chiefly through Lily that we get the last,
somewhat puzzling, minor movement. She thinks
much of Mrs. Ramsay, and she is distressed by
Mr. Ramsay's unconscious demand upon her for
the sympathy his wife had always had ready
for him. To Lily it seemed that "his immense
self-pity, his demand for sympathy, poured and
spread itself in pools at her feet, and all she
did, miserable sinner that she was, was to draw

her skirts a little closer around her ankles, lest she should get wet.'' She begins to work again upon the unfinished painting begun ten years before, and tries to recapture the glimpse of truth that was to be made clear through the relation of masses, lights, and shadows. She reflects that Mrs. Ramsay's gift had been to make of the moment something memorable; she had made life stand still for an instant and take a shape. Lily in her way was trying to do the same thing. There was this truth, this reality, which suddenly laid hands upon her, ''emerged stark at the back of appearances and commanded her attention.'' Wondering about the meaning of life, Lily thinks: ''The great revelation had never come. The great revelation perhaps never did come. Instead there were little daily miracles, illuminations, matches struck unexpectedly in the dark.'' She regains her feeling of completeness about the house and the people, the feeling that ten years ago had made her say she was in love with it. ''Love had a thousand shapes. There might be lovers whose gift it was to choose out the elements of things and place them together, and so, giving them a wholeness not theirs in life, make of some scene or meeting of people (now all gone and separate) one of those globed, compacted things over which thought lingers and love plays.'' This is at all events what Mrs. Woolf has made out of the scene and the people of *To the Lighthouse;* our thought lingers over this globed, compacted thing rather than over any individual characters.

VII

One felt more and more dubious about the Mrs. Brown of the railway carriage, when she appeared as a hero-heroine in *Orlando,* spanning the centuries from Queen Elizabeth to Thursday, October 11, 1928—at that moment aged thirty-six and a lady, though she had started out three centuries before as a young boy. It began to be clear that Mrs. Woolf was seeking to capture not characters, but life; and that perhaps the most significant sentence in her essay on "Mrs. Brown" was that one slipped in casually at the end—"for Mrs. Brown is the spirit we live by, Life itself." In capturing that spirit, characters often serve her very well, but when they don't, an empty house in the Hebrides or a mark on the wall will do. Orlando at any moment of his surprising career is no more alive than his historic house, where "the light airs which forever moved about the galleries stirred the blue and green arras, so that it looked as if the huntsmen were riding and Daphne were flying." Yet life escapes after all. When Orlando's lover swoops down in his plane on the last page, there springs up over his head a wild bird. "The wild goose," cries Orlando. It had haunted her ever since she was a child. "There flies the wild goose. It flies past the window out to sea. . . . I've seen it here, there, England, Persia, Italy . . . always it flies out to sea, and always I fling after it words like nets, which shrivel as I have seen nets shrivel, drawn on deck with only seaweed in them. And sometimes there is an inch of silver—six words—in the bottom of the net."

Realizing the nature of her aim, we begin to understand certain effects upon us of her books. Were we wholly absorbed in Jacob or Rachel or Mrs. Ramsay, we should have a desolating conviction of the futility of life when we finished their stories. We don't—at least so far as one can judge from what readers say. This is partly because, as Clive Bell says, Mrs. Woolf looks at her people through a cool sheet of glass; if she is watching a pair of lovers, she knows and puts down what they are feeling and saying. She herself feels the romance of the situation, but does not share the emotions of the actors. She is detached; and we too are detached. She can give the vision of someone feeling intensely; perhaps she shared the emotion when her imagination first projected the person and situation. But she has withdrawn from it and held it off for contemplation. Compare the experience of frustration in love that Mary, in *Night and Day,* goes through, with that of Gwenda in *The Three Sisters* or Philip in *Of Human Bondage.* One is prepared in Mary's case, as in the others, to make the usual emotional identification; the experience of emotional frustration is so common that most readers possess that key into the realm of vicarious living. But Mary's struggle and suffering move us as spectators, rather than as participants. We draw away even from our own similar experience, and are contemplative instead of warmly reminiscent.

This effect of looking through glass at a picture may be one result of a constant quality of Mrs. Woolf's style,—the concreteness of its visual imagery. Mary in the midst of her sense of defeat realizes that she will presently be able to find a certain solace in work: "Now when all was tempest and high running waves, she knew of a land where the sun shone clear upon Italian grammars and files of docketed papers. Nevertheless from the skeleton pallor of that land, and the rocks that broke its surface, she knew that her life there would be harsh and lonely beyond endurance." The example is inconclusive; the whole book is needed to test the effect. But it does illustrate the constant touch upon the visual sense. Then the ease with which Mrs. Woolf slips in and out of people's minds keeps us from ever taking up a position permanently in any one character's mind. We live in Strether's mind throughout *The Ambassadors*. We are all but drowned in Ivan Karamazov's. We never desert

Mary Olivier; if we wax philosophic, it is with her. But if we become philosophical for a moment with Mrs. Dalloway, the next instant we are outside Mrs. Dalloway, seeing her and her philosophy with the critical eye of Peter, or the slightly amused and ironic glance of Virginia Woolf. There is a constant shift of focus—from one person to another, and from individuals to life in general.

In writing of Laurence Sterne, she has perfectly expressed, as a quality of his style, what is her own as well. There are passages in her work, as in Sterne's, which bring "by the curious rhythm of their phrasing, by a touch on the visual sense, an alteration in the movement of the mind, which makes it pause and widen its gaze and slightly change its attention. We are looking out at life in general." It is because they bring these alterations in the movement of the mind that her books both keep one excited at the thought of living, and at the same time detached from living any special form of life that, if it comes to disaster, darkens the world. Here for instance is Jacob, reading Plato in his room near the British Museum: "Stone lies solid over the British Museum, as bone lies cool over the visions and heat of the brain. Only here the brain is Plato's brain and Shakespeare's; the brain has made pots and statutes, great bulls and little jewels; and crossed the river of death this way

and that incessantly, seeking some landing, now
wrapping the body well for its long sleep; now
laying a penny piece on the eyes; now turning
the toes scrupulously to the East. Meanwhile
Plato continues his dialogue; in spite of the rain;
in spite of the cab whistles; in spite of the woman
in the mews behind Great Ormond Street who has
come home drunk and cries all night long—'Let
me in!' '' Life in general: Plato and the drunken
woman in Bloomsbury; Jacob's brain, and the
brain of mankind through ages seeking a way
out of death into life. It is this life in general
with which Mrs. Woolf seeks a mode of communication. And this effort gives to her fiction
the quality she finds very rare in English fiction
—more often present in French literature—intelligence. By intelligence she means neither brilliance nor intellectual power, but ''the sense that
the interest of life does not lie in what people
do, nor even in their relations to each other, but
largely in the power to communicate with a third
party, antagonistic, enigmatic, yet perhaps per-
suadable, which one may call life in general.''
To start out with her in pursuit of Mrs. Brown—
the spirit we live by, life itself—makes one feel
as Peter did, on his way to Clarissa's party,
watching all the people leaving their houses in
evening dress, watching the footmen opening
doors: ''Everybody was going out. What with
these doors being opened, and the descent and

the start, it seemed as if the whole of London
were embarking in little boats moored to the
bank, tossing on the waters, as if the whole place
were floating off in carnival. . . ."

CHAPTER IV

THE WILD GOOSE: THE CRITIC'S

PURSUIT OF VALUES

I

In *Dead Reckonings in Fiction* the author's relation to his work had more consideration than the reader's relation to fiction. At the time it was written we had almost nothing to say about readers that was not theoretical or based on the limited experience of the critics themselves as readers. But since then, in university courses attended by students of both sexes, of ages ranging from eighteen to sixty, and of many occupations, we have gathered interesting accounts of personal experience in the reading of novels. It is no easy matter to draw forth these rather intimate revelations, because most adults who are taking college courses have definite notions of what they ought to think about books and a set of neat phrases in which to state their opinion. They feel an obligation to appreciate what is good, morally or artistically—the two often charmingly confused—and to give their reasons. So they talk facilely of plot and characterization, of what is "convincing" and what is "unreal," of "significance" or "psychology," of the author's "message," his "local color," his style, his "truth to life." One praises a book, another

119

damns the same book, and both use precisely the
same vocabulary: the characters are at once convincing and unreal, the story badly constructed
and well told. All these sharply diverse judg-
ments are expressed in phrases concerning technique that students have been taught to use by
teachers, critics and reviewers. Under the stereotyped verbal formulas lurk intimate personal reactions. Some special experience is at work in
one case, making a book emotionally or intellectually accessible; or in another, some vaguely
realized prejudice closes the book to that reader;
or perhaps some deep-seated complex of which
he cannot in the nature of things be aware makes
him love or hate the book with a fervor dispro-
portionate to any rational explanation he can
invent.

There was an intelligent young man in a University Extension course whose academic training had been interrupted by the War, but it had
left in his mind a débris of critical phrases which
he automatically used when asked his opinion of
a novel. He picked out Jack London's *Valley of
the Moon* as the best novel he had ever read.
It took a couple of weeks to discover why he
really liked that book: "Last summer," he ultimately wrote, "when recovering from an accident, I sat out in the park while a young lady read
the story aloud. A cool breeze ruffled the leaves
of the tree under which we sat, the birds sang,

the flowers were in bloom, and the lady had a voice that was pleasant to hear. Row-boats floated on the lagoon near-by, and further off I could see tennis players hopping about after a little ball, while I sat next to the charming young lady. I liked the book for the struggles of the hero. I am very fond of struggles, provided they are someone else's. The tennis players, the boaters, the children playing tag, the motorists, and the hero of the book—all were struggling. So you see I was very happy. It really is a good book, though." It was a pleasant adventure to read it.

Appreciation is not often quite so obvious as that. It may be very difficult to divine what deeply hidden chords are set vibrating within. Psychoanalysts assure us that we cannot discover our own complexes. They tell us that if we are fascinated by a writer who has a certain psychosis, we ourselves probably share that psychosis, and that is why the "release" he has achieved for himself in art gives us also satisfaction. But some romantically-minded readers, so illumined, begin to detect in themselves all sorts of delightful perversities. A young woman reads *Crime and Punishment* and in its murky light inspects her own past; for she is disturbed at her own enthusiasm over the murder and surprised at the profound sense of relief at the close of the reading. Had she always longed to see a murder—or was it possible she had craved to commit one? There had been a time some years before when she had been "very morbid"; she had wanted to be alone all the time, when not wandering about the streets; "I remembered that when I saw a dog or a cat, I would kick it, throw stones at it, torture it." Convinced that she must have been a budding Raskolnikov, she expresses her gratitude to Dostoevsky for relieving her of the heavy burden resting on what she brilliantly calls her "subconscientious" mind.

The repression that counts, in these hidden dramas of personality, is of course the one of which we are truly unconscious. But there are many aspects of our relation to a novel that we can bring into awareness and thus disengage its special significance to us. One reader enjoys *If Winter Comes* and declares the author a master of character portrayal; on deeper reflection she realizes that she read it when she was feeling "a total failure," and it made her "quite fond of herself." Her unconscious identification with the frustrated hero, who is treated so sentimentally, had made the book emotionally accessible; she enjoyed the adventure of reading it. But when she came to realize the source of her satisfaction, the adventure became an experience.

In a discussion about Somerset Maugham's *Of Human Bondage,* one disputant argued effectively enough that it was in this, that, and the other respect a poor novel; to every point made in its favor, she had a reasonable answer. But presently the real reason for her attitude to the book flashed upon her; her name was Mildred; the odiously genteel, anæmic waitress who holds the hero in degrading bondage is named Mildred. Somewhere below the threshold of her grown-up mind she resented the identification of these Mildreds. But no grown-up mind would acknowledge so childish a reason for taking a dislike to a book, until its rational defenses had been captured one after the other in the argument.

A certain book irritates me; I have to force myself to go on with it, in spite of much that engages my interest. The hero has light red whiskers, prominent pale blue eyes, and pallid freckled hands. I hate that type of masculine beauty—why, only psychoanalysis might disclose. But Hauptmann's *Fool in Christ* is in consequence almost closed to me, until I suddenly realize what is causing my aversion. Then I laugh at myself, fix my attention on the other things that interest me, and make the necessary allowance for my peculiarities of taste. But before making this trivial discovery, I had begun to find excellent reasons for considering *Fool in Christ* a poor novel. Tracking down these personal secrets may open the way to a more impersonal contemplation of values.

It is worth while to set down some of the sim-

pler conclusions to be drawn from these reading
experiences of people of diverse temperaments,
varying ages, different backgrounds; people who
exhibit every kind of psychological need; yet who
all desire to be discriminating in their reading
and critical in at least a rudimentary fashion. A
few complain that the effort at analysis destroys
their naïve pleasure in reading; not a few find
it destroying their equally naïve pleasure in themselves; some discover in it a new and delightful
way of talking about themselves—they love the
confessional and their confessions have to be
scrutinized carefully before one erects theories
of criticism upon them. Others find it interesting
and often illuminating.

The experience of the young man with Jack
London, quoted above, shows that the circumstances under which one happens to read a book
may account for the impression it makes. That
sounds utterly obvious. But it is often ignored
or forgotten when the reader turns critic. A
woman who prefers sophisticated books responded warmly to *The Growth of the Soil* because she happened to read it on her return to
New York from wide-open spaces somewhere;
and the rush of the city made life seem a meaningless jumble; so that the simple strength, order
and purpose in Isak's life satisfied a need. It
was a temporary need, not the permanent need
recorded in another comment: ''The secret rea-

son why I like *The Growth of the Soil* is that it is so restful to me to share vicariously the experience of a man who knows no inhibitions, no frustrations, no moralizing, no introspection, no analyzing—in fine, no hateful, useless waste of vitality. Isak's life is a very simple problem. Mine seems to be to me a very complex one. How heavenly to be Isak, if only for a few hundred pages." To return to special circumstances. A nurse, taking a correspondence course in fiction, found herself having to read *The Ambassadors* "to the tune of the psychopathic ward" in the hospital. "Strether's complicated brain-storms over Chad Newsome's morals were frequently interrupted by the would-be suicide who tried to tear the bandages from the throat he had failed to cut efficiently; and there was a slender pale-faced woman of forty who washed her hands and washed her hands ceaselessly." All this variety of the "real" made what the nurse called James's delicate flicking of butterflies from petals seem artificial and absurd. She criticized him for writing about unimportant experiences and not about the "roots of things." But to another woman who had just suffered a pronounced change of attitude towards life, James in *The Ambassadors* was a profoundly satisfying novelist because he pictured men and women in the throes of facing about: "I emerged refreshed and happy. It is just as when one has been trying to spell out a book in the twilight, and suddenly the lamp comes in.''

Perhaps the nurse would have found Andreyev's *Seven Who Were Hanged* more congenial reading in the psychopathic ward. It was selected by another nurse for enthusiastic praise because certain scenes were a fine expression of her own experience—such a scene as that where the father and mother of the condemned man come to see him and disturb the resignation he has painfully achieved: ''So often,'' writes the nurse, ''have I labored hours with my dying patient and finally brought him to a state of repose, when well-meaning relatives appear and spoil it all.'' An expression of one's own experience is most usually a source of satisfaction and the basis for an opinion that the ''characters are well-drawn'' and the ''plot true to life.'' Yet if the experience is one we find it painful to recall, we may condemn the novel as ''morbid.'' Another nurse was ''nauseated'' by Andreyev, as also by Dostoevsky, precisely because of all her hospital experiences with sick minds and bodies; she conjectured, perhaps rightly, that her dislike was a defense against morbid and brooding tendencies of her own. Still another reader, introspective and analytical, knowing nothing at first hand of hospitals and sick souls and the torture of confronting death, enjoyed the experiences of the fated Seven, and went on further to enjoying the daydream of herself in a similar predicament: "If I should ever have to face hanging, I believe the comparison of my emotions with those of the Seven might save me from going crazy. If someone would only arrange that I should undergo the whole thing, believing it to be real, and have me saved at the last moment, I sometimes in experimental fervor wish they would; it would be a way of finding out how my reading affect d my behaviour. But now that I have formulated such an idea, I should always suspect the sentence to be false—and that might save me, if it were real!" These rather involved speculations about herself are the source of her appreciation of this "morbid" book.

We have been led on into more complicated aspects of the reader's relation to the novel, where interpretation becomes more hazardous. Whenever a comment reveals intense dislike of a book or character, some obsession or complex may be at work, unsuspected by its owner; and we have to read between the lines and risk a guess that by a lucky chance may receive confirmation later. A young man criticized Sudermann's *Dame Care* as a third-rate novel, but he could muster few reasons for the opinion that stood their ground under questioning. It turned out that he hated Sudermann's portrait of Paul's father—as fool, or villain, or both. He realized that his attitude to the book was determined by the similarity be-

tween Paul's father and his own; he went on
talking about his father, gradually warming to
a kind of resentful defence. The father had become very like Paul's father in the end—vindictive and suffering from a sense of inferiority.
Why did he hate Sudermann's portrayal so
much? Because he loved his father? Or because he had subconsciously passed the same
judgment on him that Sudermann passes on
Paul's father and resented having it lifted into
awareness? Or possibly because he was conscious of his own resemblance to his father? At
any rate, a detached judgment on the book's mer-
its could scarcely be expected from him. He was
studying to be a librarian and would, no doubt,
often be asked to give advice to readers. Yet
he disliked having the personal and psychological
factors in criticism insisted upon; he wanted a
few firmly fixed standards. His confusion about
himself and *Dame Care* is in interesting contrast
with the clarity of a Chinese student, who preferred it above all others in a reading-list, chiefly
because it supported his own inherited conception
of life: "It has a theme, and that theme is that
extreme sacrifice is necessary in order to attain
any great object. It has much the same theme
that most of our Chinese novels have. The Chinese novel is predominantly ethical in tone. The
hero is always made to undergo all kinds of
hardships and sometimes death to attain his ob-

ject. That object might be the salvation of other persons, the betterment of society, the rescuing of one's family, or the elevation of one's nation. *Dame Care* develops its theme adequately, since every scene contains some misfortune for the hero.'' This may not take us far on the road to an impersonal evaluation of *Dame Care;* but if more critics were as clear sighted and honest with themselves as the Chinese youth, there would be less smoke and confusion in the field of criticism.

II

The discussion so far has suggested some of the very personal considerations—they may be either limitations or advantages—that must be recognized and dealt with, before the neat categories of criticism can be used—or discarded— with intelligence. But there are questions concerning the effects of fiction on the reader that are still more important for the growth of any sound theories of criticism. Is fiction escape or solution, adventure or experience, for the reader? *

The escapes furnished by fiction from certain moods and situations are often obvious enough. The young woman of cheerful temperament adores the more melancholy of Chekhov's stories,

* See Introduction, and also Ch. I. in *Dead Reckonings in Fiction.*

129

because it is so "refreshing" to experience a gloomy mood. The only daughter of elderly parents, in her longing for a brother or sister and "intimate family incidents" almost wore the covers off the Alcott books, and later delighted in *Pride and Prejudice,* becoming "absorbed in the family problems of Mrs. Bennett." But it won't do to offer family chronicles to all only children. For here is another only child— and only grandchild, with "five maiden aunts and uncles"—who always felt the Alcott families too prolific: "their sharing of experiences didn't appeal to me, who knew at all times the joy of the limelight. All large families in my childhood's list of fiction excited the sympathy that made me grateful I was not like one of these." The feeling has persisted in her adult life and she is bored with family histories, like Mann's *Buddenbrooks.* A girl who regarded herself as abused by parents, who made her practise for hours and forced Emerson and Scott upon her in her leisure moments, happened upon *Jane Eyre* and Poe, wept buckets of soothing tears, and felt justified in her belief that life was a tragedy and she was a martyr. Another reader recognized, as she looked back, that she had always read to escape the thing at hand, whatever it was; that she had been an adept at camouflaging her own dreary feelings with the local color of another's painting, and had thus avoided an analysis that might have led to a less boring environment. Years of illness had made her feel neglected and misunderstood, and she liked to read of characters who suffered and were not appreciated, but through keen intelligence finally won out. The fairy-tale of the Ugly Duckling— only slightly disguised in much grown-up fiction —is the archetype of innumerable novels that solace the ugly ducklings of life. Dostoevsky's people are not usually regarded as "delightful" and "care-free" associates, but this reader found them so in *The Idiot*: "Everyone's nerves were always at such high tension that I found myself breathless with excitement, and my heart beating much faster than its usual rate which is sometimes very slow—due to the fact that we are a small family, perhaps too reserved and quiet. Having neither brothers nor sisters on whom to vent some of my pent-up nervous energy, as I am told is done in larger families, I found an outlet in *The Idiot*."

A college boy reads and re-reads *Cyrano de Bergerac, Peter Pan,* and tales by Lord Dunsany; he thinks the ideal world would be peopled with children, that the greatest tragedy is that children grow up, and the next greatest that they want to grow up. "As for me, I shall never grow up." His favorite fiction either idealizes the child or creates a fairy-tale world, of beauty or horror; for he likes horrible tales, too, like *The*

Seven Who Were Hanged, tales so far beyond
the limits of his own life that he doesn't have
to believe in them, not really, any more than a
child believes in witches. One wonders whether,
if he continues to escape into the child's world,
he will not develop a very expert technique of
evasion that will prevent his adjustment to the
adult world. But he was young enough when
he expressed these ideas to take pleasure in a
pose. We have to decide for ourselves whether
our particular form of escape in fiction is one we
should keep on indulging. We may feel as the
reader of Poe did: "if my love of Poe means
I have the same psychosis, the pleasure I've had
is cheap at the price."

The fiction of failure may be as satisfying an
escape as that of success. Successful people take
pleasure in vicariously living through a few failures. Or people who have felt the sting of defeat,
but in some drab, dish-washing, adding-machine
atmosphere, can derive delight from really splendid failures—spectacular ones like Ivan Karamazov's, exquisite ones like Strether's in *The
Ambassadors,* romantic ones like Decoud's in
Nostromo. The dream of a splendid failure might
be consoling and congenial in moods when one of
blatant success would only disgust.

Perhaps nothing can be claimed for escapes
such as we have been discussing except a change
of mood. They are analogous to the prison psy-

chosis of which a well-known psychoanalyst *
speaks: the life prisoner often goes into a waking fantasy, and while his actual situation remains unendurable, his mood changes to one of
joy. Many people imprisoned in situations go to
books as the "lifer" goes into his waking fantasy,
and so escape from a mood, "if the writer pro-
duces a fantasy revery which the reader can accept as his own dream. Because half of life,
almost, is spent in the fantasy of dreams at night,
man is already equipped to use this false escape
method." Yet even the change of mood is not
to be denied some value as solution. A bond
salesman who had a succession of selling failures
became an omnivorous reader of detective tales.
"His vicarious success as a detective," says Dr.
Reede, "carried over into his work next day as
a feeling of success. This device took him over
a time of panic." There is no need of dwelling
longer on this point about mere change of mood.
It is hard to foretell what reading will effect a
change. Moods change for no reason and every
reason, and alter things without, or affect them
not at all.

III

To justify oneself is more permanently satisfactory than merely to escape into an imaginary

* Dr. Edward H. Reede of Washington, D. C., quoted in *Dead
Reckonings in Fiction.*

self and more congenial surroundings. And fiction is one of the most effective instruments of rationalization. Intentionally or not, readers reveal how this or that novel has made their own actions seem reasonable or inevitable, their own temperaments interesting or excusable; it has made it more possible or more delightful for them to live with themselves. Perhaps it has justified vicious attitudes as well as fine ones and confirmed unpleasant traits as well as admirable ones, though naturally the material readers offer for inspection only inadvertently discloses this reverse side.

A young man who was forced to study medicine, hated it, and abandoned it, read *The Way of All Flesh* and saw his problem in Ernest's, and his justification in Ernest's behavior. Ernest found the Church full of hypocrites—he found the medical world the same. Philip, in *Of Human Bondage,* is one of the most consoling of heroes; he makes so many false starts, suffers so frequently what the world calls failure. Yet his failures all appear to the intimate view justified and valuable. What, asks Philip's uncle, had he got from the years devoted to that art of painting he was now abandoning for medicine? And Philip, with his ironically superior air, makes precisely the response we wish we could always summon when similarly challenged. "Philip," writes a young man, "lives for me because our experiences and thoughts parallel in many instances. His ceaseless and fruitless groping for his niche in life and a satisfactory career leads him into several experiments I have already attempted. I have left college because I believed it would not lead me to any adequate occupation in after life; I have studied art in Paris and discovered my mistake; I have played with the idea of an infinite number of careers and found that my enthusiasm did not survive the realization stage, but exhausted itself in planning and expectation; just as Philip's did about going into the Church. The fact that Philip survived so many failures and finally discovered a path of comparative contentment makes me a little less hopeless on my own account."

Timid self-conscious people express great sympathy with Paul in *Dame Care*. They see their own undesirable qualities in him: his indecision, his self-pity in tortured moments, his inability to act, his fear of people whom he believes superior. But there is subtle flattery in the fact that he is the hero, and encouragement in his ultimate adjustment. "I suppose," said a girl who was an expert in the art of self-depreciation, "my great satisfaction lay in seeing that under stress Paul surmounted the obstacles in his own nature, and came out triumphantly. I have never been up against any distressful circumstances, but it was comforting to know that if the test came, someone with faults very like mine could meet it." A reader of different temperament remained quite unconvinced that Paul ultimately succeeded. To her energetic active mind, Paul was the last word in irritating incompetence, and she was sure he would continue to fail.

The part that fiction played over a period of years in the task of justification is brought out in the following experience. The writer had not wished at first to look back over her reading because it meant recalling painful episodes of her life; but in the end she found much that was clarifying in the effort. Her childhood had been shadowed by poverty and family disagreements, from which she sought relief in tales of travel, adventure, knight-errantry. Her reading was vicarious adventure, escape. Later she began to observe the lives of other people, compare them with her own, and question why "life was imposed rather than chosen." In this morose and questioning state, she sought any author who raised queries of why and wherefore, and she reveled in "long-winded monologues by characters who attempted solutions and explanations." Then she was involved in a love affair that was disastrous and disillusioning, and that sent her in search of any reading that hinted at folly similar to hers. She questioned herself, asking what immorality was, and what the responses of people in fiction had been in situations like hers.

136

She read *The Bright Shawl, Cytherea, The Secret Places of the Heart, The Lost Lady, The Genius.* At present she says that she reads, not to get away from the realities of the external world, not to seek philosophies of existence, but to probe herself and vindicate herself in her own eyes, by what authors do with their characters in fiction.

Proportionate to our satisfaction in the book that vindicates us is our violent and often obscure resentment of the book that topples over some carefully built-up structure in which we are living comfortably. *Of Human Bondage*—which provides so many readers with satisfying emotional escapes and justifications—made one reader suffer "mentally and physically." "It sickened and angered and ate into me with its red petticoat, dirty smock, crooked teeth, corn-y toes and what-not. The Philips and Miss Prices became unending nightmares. I hate ugliness. It is possible for me to accept it. Without at all understanding it, I am able to sympathize with it. But I refuse to take it to me, to make it part of my life. I have the grained-in English respect for wholesomeness and human dignity. Maugham not only destroyed my illusions regarding the world but gnawed at some of the illusions I had regarding myself. I found myself revaluing almost everything I had previously read. I have never reached a final decision. I am able to see

the nobility which grows out of bondage, of human suffering. In that light, I cannot be noble; I have been so utterly free, I can hardly say I have suffered—at least not sufficiently. But must I go looking for suffering? There is so much joy in the world. And I do not believe that a knowledge of the meagreness of life heightens one's appreciation of its goodness. For my own part, I cannot say that I have known a fuller ecstasy of being since I became aware of life's sordidness, than I knew when I raced with my dogs."
There was a Social Service worker who had great enthusiasm for her vocation. She was about to marry an engineer whose work was in a coal-mining town where there were plenty of poor people on whom she could try out, as she put it, all the pet theories she had paid for at college. She traced some of her social-service enthusiasm to her early reading of *Pollyanna* books and *Mrs. Wiggs of the Cabbage Patch* and *The Recreation of Brian Kent* (by Harold Bell Wright), and other books that dealt with broken-down lives, prostitution, desertion, and poor orphans. Now she herself was going to work with Cabbage Patch people. Her favorite fiction in the course she was taking dealt with situations and people that needed the services of a social-service diagnostician: novels by Galsworthy, Hardy, George Eliot. "I love to diagnose in fiction, from any chapter 3 on." But when the Russian novelists

came on the scene, she had a severe shock. She felt hatred and contempt for all the characters in *The Brothers Karamazov;* she loathed Gorky; she shuddered at the very mention of murder, insanity, radical, gendarme. She was able to endure *War and Peace* by regarding it as a sociological treatise against war. Now one would have thought that some of the people in these Russian novels so needed the help of a social-service expert that she would have responded with alacrity. Probably the trouble was this: she felt equal to a Galsworthy or a Hardy problem, with the equipment of her theories; but Dostoevsky was so much more searching and profound that she felt unable to cope with his situations and his characters, and sought to defend herself by hating them.

IV

There are some glimpses of the interaction between fiction and living in the experiences we have been dealing with. But they have not been those of the actively experimental readers who are likely to try out a suggestion furnished by a novel just as they would other suggestions that come to them. Such readers were not content as children to lose themselves in the delightful dream. If they have been reading *The Arabian Nights,* they prowl about the neighborhood looking for a magic door; and finding a large round

139

stone in the ground, with an iron ring, they lift it up, thrill at the glimpse of a mysterious cave, start to explore it, and have to be rescued from a fall into a disused well. A girl who belongs to a Catholic family recalls how the stories in the *Sacred Heart Messenger* fired her to missionary zeal for baptism; with her brother's assistance she was administering a fifth baptism "when the scandalized cook interrupted the service and rescued the shivering form of the convert—her grandson." "In the stories it had all been so easy; the relative would leave the dying child, or the heroine's pastor or mother would assist in the administration of the sacrament. My zeal led me to the death-beds of two completely strange neighbors, to my family's great embarrassment." A young man remembers vividly how Edward Stratemeyer's Dave Porter books inspired him to imitation. "When Dave's eyes flashed fire, I used to stand in front of the mirror to see whether I could discover any scintillations. In one of Dave's fights with the school bully, our hero banged the bully's head against the boat-house and made him see stars. I tried this at school one day, banging a fellow's head against the blackboard, but neither the victim, the teacher, nor my parents seemed to approve." He became an ardent Yale rooter, because of Frank Merriwell and Dink Stover; but never risked any money on football games—"not that I had the slightest fear of losing, for I had read so often of what a glorious thing it was to be a good loser; but because neither Stover nor Merriwell nor Dave ever gambled or smoked or drank. Nor did I—then.'' Inspired to swimming feats by one hero, he built himself up from a delicate boy into a record-breaker. *Black Beauty* made him a lover of horses and Uncle Tom a liker of negroes. ''I have tasted of Byron, and he has been my inspiration in that oldest game of all, although I have gotten a lot from De Maupassant, and wisdom from Arthur Schnitzler. And so we continue to read in living and live in reading.'' Why censorship?

Another young man gives an account of the effect upon him of boys' stories and college tales that is very similar, but the ending is strikingly different. Realizing how suggestible he was, he has refrained from exposing himself to ''suggestive'' novels, fearing they might make him do ''something wild,'' and that would be regrettable, since he is most satisfactorily engaged to a fine girl. Probably the thought of his potential wildness is as satisfying an imaginative experience as any novel would be. Few readers can recall as definite a history of imitation as these young men. The more usual experience is one of perpetual interaction between literature and life; literature now giving some impulse to living, again an actual experience leading us to literature for interpretation or justification. The interplay appears in all possible combinations and the whole process is obscure and difficult to trace as we look back upon it. Yet the moralist and the censor would like to sum it all up in the simple question: will people act upon the suggestions of fiction? And they often risk an affirmative answer, relying on a few instances that furnish no basis for generalization, and on some convenient rough-and-ready psychological theory. One of the most promising statements of the complex problems involved in an answer to that simple question is made by I. A. Richards, in his *Theory of Literary Criticism.* In trying to set some standard of value for the art experience, he assumes that the most valuable states of mind are those which involve the widest and most comprehensive coördination of activities, and the least curtailment, conflict, starvation, and restriction. He talks much of what he calls attitudes. A work of art coördinates a number of our impulses, for example; no overt action may take place; but incipient or imaginal action is as important as overt action, though its results are not immediately apparent. These incipient activities or tendencies to action he calls attitudes. An experience may be made up of incipient promptings, lightly stimulated tendencies to acts of one kind or another, faint preliminary preparations to do this or that. Emotions are the signs of attitudes; it is the attitudes themselves that are the all-important part of any experience. "It is not the intensity of the conscious experience, its thrill, its pleasure, or its poignancy which gives it value, but the organization of its impulses for freedom and fulness of life. There are plenty of ecstatic instants that are valueless; the character of consciousness at any moment is no certain sign of the excellence of the impulses from which it arises. . . . A more reliable but less accessible set of signs can be found in the readiness for this or that kind of behavior in which we find ourselves after the experience." Fiction has done much to develop conventional, stereotyped, "stock" attitudes, towards friendship, country, love, self-sacrifice, and so forth. Such attitudes tend to become fixed at certain levels of development, unless the pressure of experience or an unusual capacity for critical reflection operate to change them. When literature or art helps to fix immature attitudes, it may leave the adult worse, not better, adjusted to the possibilities of his existence than a child; for he is facing fictions projected by his own stock responses. Such art and literature Mr. Richards calls "bad." "Against these stock responses the artist's internal and external conflicts are fought, and with them the popular writer's triumphs are made." It is true that people seldom imitate directly what they see in the moving-picture or read in

143

the best-seller. If they did, the effects would be obvious and easily dealt with. There may be no resemblance and no discernible connection between the experience due to a work of art and the later behavior and experience which is affected by it. The influence may be overlooked or denied, but not, insists Mr. Richards, "by anyone who has a sufficient conception of the ways in which attitudes develop." When a novel or a poem or a play has given more than usual order and coherence to our responses—has organized our impulses more completely and on a higher level than we usually achieve—we have a feeling of relief, freedom, increased competence. "We seem to feel that our command of life, our insight into it, and our discrimination of its possibilities, is enhanced, even for situations having little or nothing to do with the subject of the reading." If on the other hand, our organization is depressed, forced to a lower and cruder and more wasteful level, we feel dissatisfied or baffled.

A more eloquent expression of much the same idea is worth quoting from a comment on Dostoevsky's *Crime and Punishment* by a student, Mrs. Emily M. F. Cooper. "Good literature will call out the greatest number of unsatisfied tendencies, all crying to be used. It will call them out fully and in repeated, varying ways. It will call them out with vividness and realism, giving them the

144

fullest and most exquisite satisfaction. . . . Conversely, the 'bad' in literature will draw upon only a few, perhaps one, of the instincts or tendencies or factors of the psychological equipment. It will draw upon them only partially and superficially and quite undisguisedly. In its crudeness it will have no semblance to the complexity of real life and therefore will give only temporary satisfaction, and will lack the ability to intensify life or give the sense of full living. It will not work on them vividly or powerfully and will be as unsatisfying as slight exercise of a muscle requiring full use. There is then a distinct relation between good literature and an intricately developed psychological equipment, both on the part of the author and the reader. . . . Let us take Dostoevsky's *Crime and Punishment.* Dostoevsky himself was a man of deep-seated instinctive and emotional equipment, with a highly developed nervous organization, high intelligence and wide social and philosophical interests. Therefore his work should and does draw upon a bewildering source of material and elicits a bewildering reaction. . . . *Crime and Punishment* plays on the theme of murder, the motives of murder, the philosophy of murder, play thoughts of murder, the desire of murder, the fear of murder, murder in its effect upon the murderer, murder in its social effect. Murder alone is probably based on the self-assertive instinct, and the

145

underlying idea of the book, that a superman may commit murder and escape its consequences, also appeals to the assertive impulse. Raskolnikov's self-surrender during the course of the book and his ultimate acceptance of the futility of the theory he held at first appeals strongly to the submissive impulse, the balance wheel of the assertive. But in the course of the book, these two instincts and their emotions are so involved with other instincts and emotions acting and counteracting that one could never say they are the dominant reactions elicited. Some readers may be attracted to the murder theme because it satisfies the curiosity motive, curiosity as to what it would be like to commit murder; some may enjoy it because it has the elements of a detective tale and satisfies another form of the mastery impulse —planned murder and escape. The sex motive— the old reliable—appears in the novel in Raskolnikov's love for Sonia and her trade of prostitution. These are some of the instincts at play in the book, but so counter-balanced and complicated by others that a real semblance to the complexity of life is attained. Feeling tones, likes and dislikes, emotions, interests, tendencies and counter tendencies are woven in and out in a vast close fabric. Murder is the theme, but the whole of life comes to support it, to play upon it, to light it up, to explain it, to arouse it completely, to present it with verisimilitude. Almost the whole catalogue of human impulses is drawn into it. And the skill, which arouses the critical, intellectual motive of mastery and manipulation, is its crowning glory to the acute and well-trained. . . . Dostoevsky epitomizes life in the full, life to its nth degree of activity, life lived that way, longed for that way, and life reproduced that way. That is why he is so bewildering, so fascinating, so excruciating and withal so satisfying; because he packs into one moment a multitude of reactions and his novels cover months and years of those moments; because all of these native desires are satisfied not only in the person of one, but of many characters, each exhibiting and eliciting reactions in every possible phase and nuance. And so do we 'play' with Dostoevsky.''

If we accept this theory—that the work of art is valuable in proportion to the value of the experiences it gives us; and if we test that value by our readiness for this or that sort of behavior after the experience, we are then faced with a question not discussed by Mr. Richards. What is the test of value in behavior? The answer depends upon our philosophy of life, our ethical standards, our conception of the desirable form and development of society—and on about everything else. We may share Mr. Richards' prepossession in favor of ''freedom and fulness of Life,'' and think we are moving in that direction and are developing finer and finer attitudes. And an observer with a different philosophy may think we are going to the dogs and corrupting the social order. Suppose we illustrate the difficulty from an account of a reading experience covering a number of years. The writer was a woman in her early thirties, just completing a course in journalism, after having been a nurse and social worker for some eight years. As a child she cared nothing for reading; and in college her taste was for the explanatory and argumentative. She specialized in science and liked to dissect and analyze everything. Later she read little but nursing and medical journals and such magazines as *The Survey* and *The Nation*. When she was twenty-six or twenty-seven, she was a guest one summer at the home of an author. The chief furnishings of the house were books, and the room she occupied had evidently, she said, been arranged for a man—being supplied generously with "sex books." She found Galsworthy's *Dark Flower* first, then Lawrence's *Women in Love*, then *Jurgen* and *Casanova*. Any society for the Suppression of Vice would now regard her as doomed. She would not have made the effort to secure these novels, of which she had heard, but finding them there, all assembled, rather delighted her, and she read fast. For the first time sex relationships appeared to her in their emotional rather than their scientific aspect. From this primary interest and satisfaction, her pleasure spread to other phases of the books and

148

the long dormant taste for reading developed. It had been dormant, she believed, because for years, as a nurse, she had been the confidant of other people, and the desire for contact and vicarious experience had been satisfied.

Her revulsion against the sort of reading she had formerly liked was pronounced; all efforts to teach, point morals, propagandize irritated her; the place for that was the editorial page or the social service magazine, not the novel. Before that, the only fiction she liked was that with a pronounced social purpose. Once she began to read widely, her own varied experience in district nursing on the East Side in New York increased her appreciation of types and situations in fiction. She found Anne Parrish's *Perennial Bachelor* convincing, because of her hospital memories of elderly spinsters whose unacknowledged desire had always been for a baby, and who saw what had always been a remote possibility cut off for good by incurable disease. "Invariably incidents in books like this make me go back and recapture pictures in life." And the process works the other way, too. As a result of reading, episodes and people on the East Side "fall into definite patterns of tragedy, comedy, or farce."

Books, she was convinced, had influenced her actions, as well as her attitudes. "Being New England and Catholic, I was habitually quite narrow generally. Contacts and friendships in life have done more than books to liberate me, but books have done much. . . . I secretly admire him who blasphemes, because I never dared do it until it was too late to acquire the habit or enjoy it; I enjoy hearing persons too smug in their righteousness examined and criticized, and after the first shock I go back and enjoy hearing it again. While this type of reading increases my enjoyment, it could not affect my actions, because once we have acquired habits, we are miserable in changing, even though we admire the other way." (If, however, attitudes—"faint preliminary promptings to do this or that"—are as important as Mr. Richards maintains, she may be surprised by her own actions some day or other.) Reading has increased her tolerance, convincing her that what one man does may be sinful, but the same act may be virtue in another. She likes odd and even vicious people in fiction as well as in life; clumsy, rude people in fiction remind her that "she may have bathed just as unattractive persons in the hospital wards; but they were always interesting. It is never what they do which makes me like people in books or in life—it is how they do it and what went before in life to make them as they are."

To some, this will seem a very fine attitude; if fiction helped to develop it, it is "good" fiction. To others it will seem a distressingly unmoral attitude, the fiction that influenced it "bad," and the last state of that reader worse than the first, when she was "New England and Catholic." It is interesting to compare this rather ingenuous account with a more varied and subtle expression of the interplay of life and fiction in the development of a mature personality. The writer goes back to her early pleasure in *Alice in Wonderland*: "It always had the power of carrying me down the rabbit-hole and through Alice's adventures with a sense of reality far greater than that attached to many actual experiences. Finishing *Alice* and many another book since, was like being dropped from another planet, so strange and alien seemed the everyday world about me upon my return from my world of illusion. From the time I was nine till I was fifteen I read everything I could lay my hands upon, including Shakespere, the Bible, the cook's dream-book, Thackeray, Dickens, the family doctor-book, and many novels, and they all fed a little understood but acutely felt curiosity and hunger. I was eager for experience, both actual and vicarious. As a child I found the world of illusion or make-believe more real and necessary to me much of the time than the actual world; so that adjustment was difficult and often painful. Increasing experience and careless grown-ups gradually stripped me of my high confidence in the beauty and goodness of the world. With the approach of adolescence and the definite response to religious teaching, I became more aware of the darker side of life and more and more lost my happy confidence in it and my own adequacy to cope with it. The most profound effect of my religious training was a conviction that I was a miserable sinner and there was no escape. From this time on there was a heavy feeling of guilt for every moment of irresponsible joy. During the years from fifteen to twenty books and the world out-of-doors were my great solace and I fled to them for forgetfulness and comfort. The books transported me from the disappointing world where I found myself and nature poured out upon me a comfort which held some unrecognized suggestion of renewed confidence in life. At that time I preferred tragic tales, and read and re-read the most heart-breaking of Shakespere's, identifying myself with all the characters who suffered. I died with the little princes in the Tower, committed murders with the Macbeths, died of love and poison with Romeo and Juliet; and any novel with an unhappy ending was indelibly imprinted on my consciousness, and I carried about with me for days the atmosphere of incurable sadness. As I look back at that time I see myself living a sort of dual existence, clinging desperately to a world of illusion, all beauty and goodness on the one hand, and on the other being thrust into an actual world of ugly sordidness and disappointing people.

"Then for many years I seem to have given over the struggle and to have turned the key on this troubled inner life of futile questioning and protest, and to have accepted grudgingly the sorry terms on which life was offered me. I filled my days with physical activities and my nights with sleep, and if in quiet moments I fancied rumblings behind my locked door, I read feverishly— dull facts or novels with happy endings. Though I lived a very full and busy life, completing a strenuous professional training, marrying and bearing two children, it was all done with my back to the locked door, and I was very busy and gay and seemed to forget its existence completely. When a few years ago my health and my marriage disintegrated simultaneously, the inevitable and long-delayed adjustment could no longer be postponed. About this time I stumbled on *Jean-Christophe,* and in it I found so deep an insight into human emotion and experience, so profound an understanding of the weakness and incompleteness of even the noblest souls, that dimly and gradually I was able to break through my unhappy isolation and arrive presently at a sense of release from my oppressive consciousness of moral guilt. A new confidence in life and in myself flowed back upon me." Among books of recent reading that affected her strongly, she mentioned *Mary Olivier* and *Sons and Lovers.* She lived very fully through Mary's experience

—her childish need of love, her tingling awareness of the beauty and poignancy of the outer world, and her frightening glimpses of the shadows in the grown-up lives about her. In these respects she shared Mary's emotions till they seemed her own, become articulate. "While *Mary Olivier* represents to me a sort of pattern of my own life as I should like to have lived it, much of *Sons and Lovers* corresponds rather closely to that which has been distressingly obscure, muddled and frustrated in my own experience." Summing it up, "books have meant to me companionship, escape, pleasure, beauty, finger-posts, searchlights, and occasionally hairshirts and dust and ashes on my head."

Most of the purposes served by novels in the lives of readers are apparent here: their value as a statement of one's own experience; as a dream of what we should like to be—and may possibly be encouraged to become; as an outlet for moods and emotions; an excuse for self-pity; a device for evasion; an instrument for the clarification of conflicts and problems. It is this last purpose that the psychologist would regard as the most important.

VI

No man, says the psychologist we have already quoted, can as a rule define his own conduct except in terms of his reactions to outside situa-

154

tions; he sees the struggle as a war between himself and something outside, whereas the psychologist sees it as something internal, a conflict between warring selves. The man projects it into situations, dramatizes it. Fiction helps him to do that, whether he is the creator or the consumer of the novel. But all the while he is absorbed in the dramatization, he is aware—perhaps clearly, perhaps very obscurely—that the problem is really within; and that brings him back more prepared to confront his own inner self. The particular problem dramatized may not be exactly analogous to his own. But all except the most unimaginative have a dexterity of mind that enables them to perform the feat of transference. "Just as in chess we may imagine it as a military game, or a tour d'amour, or what not; so the same story can be used for different problems." We play a mental chess game, using impersonated realities as gambits. Sometimes the game is played to a successful conclusion; we are elated; "and the elation of success often means that the intellect finds the thing next day in the sensible mind as a working plan." But often the problems of fiction are not solved; the conflict eventuates in madness, suicide, disillusion. That—with readers who have reached a certain level of development—makes no difference, if they have come to see what the problem involves and what forces are in conflict. There has been illumina-

155

tion, if not solution. Take, for example, this experience with *The Brothers Karamazov:* "For several years I had been troubled, confused in my own mind, unhappy, groping. In some degree I had worked my way partly through the maze of certain problems and questions which had been baffling me, but much was obscured by clouds of uncertainty and doubt which I had not enough mental ability to clear away. When I read the chapter, *The Grand Inquisitor,* the scales fell from my eyes, and religion, as it is presented to and practised by the weak, stood forth in all its ugli-ness. The traditions of years crumbled away like the Palace of Beauty in *Parsifal,* and the stones still lie where they fell. My landscape and horizon grew more distinct; what had been blurred was clarified. Ivan gathered up all my vague attempts at a philosophy of life and crys-tallized them. It was like stepping out from a darkened room into a spring morning with its teeming possibilities." And apparently Ivan's ultimate disasters could not destroy the effect of this enlightenment.

Nor does Tolstoy's *War and Peace*—"The greatest novel I have ever read"—offer what is usually called a solution to a young man who re-quires of an author that "he explain and console by the plights of others—and that he give me re-laxation from the strain of sustained effort by showing me the inevitable end of everything human." It is the process of adjustment that Tolstoy's characters go through that satisfies him: "The molten flux flows back and forth; in a sudden swirl it emits brilliant sparks; the colors on its surface are continually changing. But the heat begins to decrease, the motion to become more sluggish, the color becomes neutral, and finally crystallization takes place. So with Natasha, Princess Marya, Pierre, Nikolai. But even as their adjustment becomes complete, in Nikolenka the entire process is beginning over again. What can I say of such a novel? True, my problem is not permanently solved, but I have secured something I can carry away, to which I can refer for added courage, which can help me to comprehend."

VII

And the conclusion?

Perhaps this reading may suggest something to you.

INDEX

INDEX

161

INDEX